D0180710

Bear With Me

The Biography of

Dennis Patrick "Doc" Casey

By Don Theye

ISBN 0-913062-22-7

Dedicated to
Pauline Foley, "Ma Bear",
a remarkable woman and mother
who was always there.

Thanks to the Caseys
for their trust and confidence,
to Mary Roth DDS for setting me straight
that one does not "yank" a tooth,
one extracts the tooth,
to BY, who thought I was a good writer,
until he edited my manuscript.

A special thanks to my amigo,
Jon Crane for permission to use his painting
from County Cork, Ireland, "Emerald Way".

*The art of Jon Crane may be viewed on the
internet at www.joncranewatercolors.com*

Don Theye

CONTENTS

Mill Iron 1

Family and Farm 5

Carroll College 21

Creighton - Class of 1955 .25

Social Life at Creighton 31

Pickstown and Pauline 33

Guam 37

Rapid City and Beyond 41

Bear Country USA 49

Behind the Scenes 59

Cowhand 61

Obsessions 65

Who? 69

Celebrities 71

Confrontation 73

Progeny 77

Goin' Home 89

Epilogue 97

Ancestry 99

The Author 104

"To live is the rarest thing in the world.
Most people exist, that is all."

– Oscar Wilde

FOREWORD

In August 2000, Sean Casey, asked if I would come to Bear Country USA to look at the expansion of the animal "Babyland" compound, and share some of my thoughts on the project. While we casually strolled around the area, Sean pointed out some of the compounds attractions, where the bear cubs would be, a special place for wolf cubs near the new waterfall, the landscaping, fences, visitor area, amphitheater and more.

We stopped at a small, quiet knoll shaded with towering Ponderosa Pines. Sean paused and was quiet for a moment. His eyes became misty as he said, with obvious respect, "This is where the memorial for Doc will be placed. It occurred to me then and later that none of the Casey's referred to their father as Dad, always Doc, and always with respect. Sean spoke of his father and mother, the beginning of Bear Country USA, the trailer on the hill where they lived during the summer months years ago, experiences with the animals, how he and his brothers and sister were raised in this environment, and more. The more he talked, the more my curiosity was aroused. It was soon obvious that this was no ordinary family and Doc Casey was, by no means, an ordinary person.

Toward the end of the day, I casually remarked to Sean that someone should write a book about Doc, the Casey's and Bear Country. A few days later, I met again with Sean, and later with members of the family. They asked if I would be interested in taking on the project. I agreed to try and write the biography of Doc Casey. It has probably been one of the most interesting year's of my life, getting to know Doc Casey through the eyes and words of others. I did not know Doc while he lived but I feel that I have come to know him through his family, his friends and some of those with whom he was not so friendly.

Dennis Patrick "Doc" Casey was an enigma. In his lifetime, he touched the lives, spirits and funny-bones of many people in many ways, be they princes or paupers, politicians or priests, moguls or miners. He had a special gift of doing so on a level field of equality with but one rule, "play the game of life for the love of the game, not the damn score!".

People were either amused or confused, or both, where Doc was concerned. More often than not, his family was often at a loss as to how they should treat, entertain, converse and satisfy his inquiring mind and entrepreneurial spirit. With him there was no mincing of words. A spade was indeed a spade. Whenever one of his kids or an employee would screw up in any number of ways, Doc, instead of "chewing" them out, he would look them in the eye, shake his head a couple of times and simply ask, "Well, did 'ya learn anything?" And they did.

Were you to ask anyone who had the good fortune of meeting Doc Casey, regardless of what else may be said, that grin would always come up. It was difficult to know for certain just what lay beneath the sparkling surface of that grin but clearly, it was an honest grin deserving of mention. It was, no doubt, this sort of grin that inspired the title and lyrics for that fine old Irish song, "When Irish Eyes Are Smiling."

Essential to the telling of this story are several direct quotes from but a few of the people who knew Doc, each a thread or "yarn", if you will, without which the "Doc" tapestry could not had been woven. I accumulated many stories about Doc. Once it was learned that I was writing Doc's biography, people would approach and share with me their personal stories regarding him. I regret that many of these are not included, but they served to confirm what has been written herein. The Casey Clan and I thank everyone for what they shared with us in words, deeds, thoughts and prayers.

There will be references to copious amounts of alcohol consumption and cigarette smoking. These are not intended as judgmental. Too often, in western society, we tend to judge lifestyles deemed unsuitable by a small band of conservative "people judgers" whose only standard is that everyone must be perfect according to their own interpretation of society and religion. In this cocoon spun from threads of negative criticism and categorical judgments, they lose sight of the human qualities of honesty, generosity and self reliance. Jack Casey, Doc's older brother, who still lives on the family farm in Mitchell, South Dakota, summed it up just fine. "We all got troubles with something now, don't we?"

Don Theye
Rapid City, South Dakota
April 2002

Doc Casey stopped his dented, grimy pickup on the highest rise of the Mill Iron ranch. He switched the ignition key off, shifted to neutral, set the hand brake and plucked a cigarette out of a crumpled, nearly empty pack of Kools. He placed the butt between his lips noticing that he had the wrong end in his mouth. Turning it, he grunted, struck a match then lit up and pulled the smoke deeply into his lungs, wincing at the irritation it caused.

Sitting awhile longer he let his gaze slowly take in the land, his land. An early spring rain encouraged the new grasses in thick mats of pale green, contrasting sharply with the dark needles of the Ponderosa pines and patches of winter killed grasses. Smiling to himself and God, Doc slowly opened the door of the pickup and eased out of the seat to stand on the ground, careful not to step on a newly opened Pasque Flower. His left pant leg was half tucked in the top of a scuffed, dusty cowboy boot but Doc paid it no mind.

Doc had a personal love for this land and with this part of South Dakota. His breathing was shallow as he walked to a limestone outcropping on the rise, catching a brief glimpse of several Mule Deer bounding over a distant hill and into a thick stand of pines to the east. Reaching the outcropping, he leaned against its rough surface warmed by the late morning sun. Again, his eyes took in the vast panorama before him. He felt somewhat better now.

The southern hills sloped downward to meet the high plains, as barren as the **MILL IRON** Mill Iron is lush. And all around, Doc spotted his cattle, a lazy herd of twenty or thirty buffalo, and in the distance a small band of elk. Pecking away at fresh cattle droppings and buffalo dung, the Magpies competed for the embedded grass and weed seeds.

A wisp of a breeze blended together the fresh scent of pine and cedar trees along with a touch of new Cottonwood leaves. Doc carefully extinguished his cigarette in a crevice in the rock. It was the kind of a day he enjoyed and he was, without a doubt, standing in the place where he wanted to be. He said, softly, to himself, "this is what I worked for. This has meaning." He remained by the outcropping for a time then, with a sigh, turned and went to his truck. As he did, his head was filled with his land, his family, his roots, and how he came to be where he was. These thoughts sustained him until he reached the main road and headed north to Bear Country, and later to his home in Rapid Valley where Pauline would be waiting.

Doc Casey's roots were planted deep in the sod of Ireland. His great-grandfather, John O'Grady Sr. was born in County Cork and emigrated to America at a time when thousands of his countrymen were doing the same. They left the Emerald Isle, following a rainbow of hope, hoping to find at its end their personal pot of gold. Most of them would be content with a job, a couple of potatoes and a place to call a home of their own. Many became successful in a variety of skills and professions utilizing a strong work ethic to turn hope into reality.

John O'Grady Sr. went west to Galena, Illinois where he met and married Ellen Halloran. Encouraged by reports of land opportunity in the Midwest USA, he migrated to Dixon County, Nebraska in 1872-1873 and began homesteading on an allotment of 160 acres. Their first home was a dugout cave with a stick and sod roof. Later, on that very spot, they built a frame house of hand-hewn timbers. This area would later become known as Tara Hill.

From the union of John and Ellen came thirteen children. Their daughter, Ellen O'Grady, married Maurice Casey. One of their four boys would be Edward James Casey who married Agnes Isabelle Kappenman who gave birth to seven children, Dennis Patrick Casey was the second youngest. There is, unfortunately, no history for the family of Maurice Casey.

Agnes Casey was the daughter of John Kappenman and Theresa Holden. John's father and mother were John Kappenman Sr. and Amelia Brown, both born in what was then Prussia (Germany). They immigrated to America and eventually Illinois. Here, they met and were married on 28

FAMILY AND FARM

September 1856. In April 1870, they moved to Dakota Territory and took up a half section of land as their homestead and timber claim. John and Amelia had fourteen children, one of which was John Ceriak Kappenman, Dennis "Doc" Casey's grandfather.

Edward J.Casey, Doc Casey's father, was one of four boys born to Maurice Casey and Ellen O'Grady. When the boys, Dennis (Doc's uncle), Jack, Ed and Maurice Jr. were between four and ten years old they were separated. Maurice and Ed went to live on their Grandfather O'Grady's farm near O'Neill, Nebraska along with their mother and a baby sister, also named Ellen, who died young. Jack and Dennis were placed in Mercy Orphanage in Omaha, Nebraska but were soon adopted by two families in Greeley, Nebraska.

Maurice Jr. later went to live with an aunt in Sioux City, Iowa. Meanwhile, Uncle Cornelius, "Cud", came to live on the O'Grady farm and remained there after Grandfather O'Grady died. He was a tough, cantankerous old guy and difficult to get along with. Ed decided to leave at that time. Ed had a pony that he grew up with, a gift from his Grandfather O'Grady. He took the pony, a small trunk with what possessions he had, and started down the road, begging for room and board until he came to Dixon, Nebraska and was befriended by Joe Lane who operated a Livery Barn. Joe gave Ed a job hauling manure for room and board plus fifty-cents a day for his hard work.

Later Ed, and his friend, Charlie Flynn, went to Barber School in Sioux City, Iowa. Completing that, they looked about for a town without a barbershop. This led them to Dolton, South Dakota where they set up their barbering business in the back of a bar and pool hall. It was in Dolton that he met Agnes Kappenman, his future wife. Shortly after Ed and Agnes were married, they moved to Mitchell, South Dakota.

In 1930, the Casey's scraped together enough money to buy 160 acre watermelon farm near Mitchell, South Dakota, moving there with their five children, Jack, Ed, Delores, Jerome and Virginia. Doc was born and raised on the farm. The Casey's became a part of the community and attended the Holy Family Catholic Church. All of the Casey children graduated from Notre Dame High School in Mitchell. During World War II, Doc and his sister, Jan, who was also born in Mitchell, attended Garfield, a country school near the farm. Both she and Doc rode Shetland Ponies to Garfield.

The classes were small at Garfield, only five students, two of them Caseys. The other three students were a little smarter than Doc or Jan providing a challenge to work harder in school then they ever had. They returned to Notre Dame Academy when Doc was in grade nine and Jan was in grade seven. Jan would remark at a later time, "My God, I thought we were way ahead of the 'kids in town'!"

These were the Depression years, just beginning when Doc Casey was born on the sixth of January 1931, weighing in at 13 pounds. Childbirth was difficult for Agnes. Already a frail person, she had been ill off and on with what was later diagnosed as diabetes. In September 1932, the youngest and last child born into the Casey family, Janice, weighed 12 pounds at birth. Eventually, Agnes' sight, as a result of her diabetes, would deteriorate to where she could not see to thread a needle. In 1953, she could not see well enough to renew her driver's license. If you did not have wheels on the farm, you had problems. Through it all, hard times or not, Ed and Agnes managed to raise their brood as best as some and better than most.

Living on the farm in the 1930's had some advantages. A vegetable garden kept the family in fresh produce. Each August and September many hands were kept busy canning vegetables that would sustain the Casey's through the winter months. Jan recalls, that having the smallest hands, she could pack pickles in jars far better than Delores or Dennis, and that her mother would heap praises on her for that singular accomplishment. Agnes had a way of conning the kids into several hours work and make it seem like fun.

Most of their livestock, cows and pigs, they raised were usually sold for money to run the farm, buy clothes, staples and condiments. The main meat diet at the Casey table was beef. On one particular occasion, there was an unexpected beef harvest when Doc and brother Jack were milking cows after a normal fourteen hour day of making hay. The cow that Jack was milking kept twitching her tail to shoo away the pesky flies. Jack, irritated, picked up his milk stool, swung it in a wide arc, hitting the cow squarely between the eyes. The cow promptly keeled over, dead. Ed, Jack and Doc got out the block and tackle and spent the night butchering the cow.

The meat meals were sometimes supplemented by an occasional pheasant or cottontail rabbit, of which there was an abundance on the farm. Doc lost his taste for pheasant but the tasty meat of cottontail rabbit would always be a favorite. Later, he developed a real liking for the meat of buffalo and elk that he raised.

The Casey family may have been poor in the economic sense but they had wealth in family values. Doc said some years later, "Hell, everybody was poor then so we didn't really know the damn difference! At least, we were eating." Everyone in the family, young and old, worked hard on the farm. It seemed that there was an enormous amount of never ending daily chores needing to be done. Ed and the older boys worked morning to night to keep everything together.

The infamous "dust bowl" years were rightly named, a continuing drought that forced many Midwestern families to vacate and lose their farms. The Casey farm was not spared as the fine grained windblown dirt formed drifts up to the top of fence posts and sifted through the smallest openings in the house. Ed was close to shutting down and leaving when the idea of planting trees in rows to form shelter belts arose. Some farmers were given government subsidies to establish the plantings. The first attempt did not succeed but the concept was workable and he tried again, this time the saplings took root. Ed was a pioneer in shelter belt planting, now a common practice on farms. Many of Ed's original trees still stand on the Jack Casey farm.

Agnes' territory was inside the farmhouse cleaning, canning, sewing, washing, ironing, tending to cuts and bruises, taking care of the children when they would get sick, packing school lunches and seeing that meals were prepared and served to a hungry brood each day. Doc would speak with loving reverence about his mother, her patience, and seemingly never ending work, all for her family. He would later remind his own family that their Grandma Agnes was always the peacemaker that encouraged her children to do better, her kitchen-table chats with them and her uncompromising love for her life partner, Edward. From the beginning, Agnes would be the binding force that kept the family together. Both Agnes and Ed were Catholics. Doc would often refer to his dad as an "earthy" Catholic (whatever that meant) and his mom a "churchy" Catholic.

The family attended mass each week at Holy Family Catholic Church. Sitting through what seemed an eternity of Hail Marys and Amens did not interest Doc at all. The ritualistic chanting and repetitive sermons, inspiring as they might have been to some of the adults, only fed his boyhood boredom and he would often nod off only be abruptly awakened by his dad sharply tweaking his ear. Doc dutifully said the Rosary every day although he would have much rather been outside.

First Communion was another one of those ceremonious things that irked Doc, as well as his sister, Jan. The idea of Communion was not so bothersome but it was the fact that each child had to stay on a white chalk line. Jan echoed Doc's feelings when she said that her memories of Communion were certainly not very Catholic or Christian because so much emphasis was placed on the fact that one had to walk a straight line. Both of them, whenever they could, did their best to walk anything but straight lines in their energetic lives.

As busy as he was, Ed kept a firm grip on family discipline never letting the children forget the basics of being a good person, a good citizen, a member of the family. He was very issue oriented, very focused. For him, it was simple: "Don't lie or cheat and you'll get by all right." He was very firm on this - there were no other options. "God helps those who help themselves." Not original but effective. "Honor your father and mother." They did. They still do.

Ed dished out a recipe of quotes, maxims and truisms blending the bible and the Old Farmer's Almanac. Words of wisdom, some with impacting originality, never left doubt as to their meaning, such as, "You burn your ass and you sit on the blister!". The senior Casey was not without a sense of humor. Even in the toughest times, he maintained his rich, sustaining sense of humor that would smooth out the bumps in life.

Ed landed a job on President Roosevelt's brainchild, Work Projects Association (WPA) driving a team of work horses on road building jobs. He was earning a whopping $48.00 a month, not much by today's standards but in the thirties it was a fair wage and enough to supplement what little the Casey farm provided through the sale of their livestock. It was hard work with long dusty hours.

It can be rightly said that there was little or no time for "quality" family sharing and togetherness. It was a life of work, sacrifice, cash money for goods bought and "hand me down" clothes. There just was not enough time to become involved in outside activities as there is today. Family life then was farming at its best, everybody sharing in whatever had to be done to assure that the family remained solid while not sacrificing their pride and well being. It was a formula comprised of one part caring and one part sharing, the end result of which would be in each of the Casey kids as they grew into adulthood.

At that time America produced strong individuals ingrained with the fundamentals of right and wrong. People had respect for family and recognized the value of education, even if only to become educated in the necessary lessons of reading, writing and arithmetic. Many did not go beyond the eighth or ninth grade but nevertheless became successful in their lives because they learned the lessons of life in that era. Ed Casey did not go beyond the third grade as a matter of fact. Because he paid attention to the three R's rigidly taught in those days, he had a good head for numbers coupled with a sense of speculation that made him successful as time went on.

He realized early on that if his kids were to succeed in the world, they had to go far beyond his third grade schooling. It was his goal to make this happen, and he did, with the enthusiastic backing of Agnes. She would do whatever it took to make sure that her kids had a good education. Unlike some of her age group, education was important for females. She would say, "No matter what, be independent and able to make a good living". All of the Casey kids went on to higher education, and each of them put their own stamp of success in their chosen advocation and profession. Meanwhile, while growing up, they each had their childhood incidents, happiness, disappointments and mishaps.

When Doc was four years old, his mother was returning from her weekly shopping trip in town, driving the family 1928 Model A. Doc and his sister, Delores (Dee) who was four years older, ran out to meet Agnes. Doc slipped on the gravel in the driveway and fell in front of the Model A. Agnes stopped the car with the right rear wheel on top of Doc's foot. She jumped out and without hesitation somehow lifted the wheel. Doc crawled out, unscathed. His first words were, "did you bring me any candy?" One of many of his narrow escapes over the years that helped earn him the title of, "One of the luckiest people alive."

At six years old, he was given the responsibility of additional chores on the farm. His first tasks were tackled with enthusiasm. He gathered the eggs and fed the pigs, morning and night, cleaned out the pig pen and chicken coops when needed and brought in buckets of water for his mother, or more like half buckets, about as much as a six year old boy could carry.

When he was seven, Doc was laying on the cellar door complaining of a belly ache. He was taken to the family doctor, Doctor Delaney who, after some prodding and poking, took Doc to the hospital and removed his appendix. Doctor Delaney's bill was paid just as all of the Casey's medical and dental bills were paid at the time, with chickens, turkeys and fresh produce.

Life was not all work on the farm. As a very young boy, Doc learned to shoot a .22 rifle. He, and his brother, Jack, put plenty of rabbit and pheasant meat on the Casey table. The .22 was indirectly the source of a couple of incidents in regard to livestock accidents. One day, Doc was plinking at crows perched atop the fence in a pen, where some horses and pigs were mixed in together. One of the shots ricocheted and hit a pig's leg, breaking it. Ed Casey later noticed that this particular pig had a bad limp and told the boys, "They'd best get those damn horses out of the pig pen 'cause it looks like one of them stepped on the pig's leg . . ."

Doc and Jack were the source of many sibling shenanigans on the Casey farm, like when they were shooting across the pasture at tree branches and one shot went clean through a milk cow's ear leaving a neat round hole. The cow just twitched the ear, no more than if it had been pestered by a fly. Many years later, Jack was visiting Doc at his home in Rapid Valley. Doc's herd of registered Angus cattle were grazing out in the pasture. The brothers were preparing to do some deer hunting up in the Black Hills and were carrying their rifles out to the car when Jack said, "Ya' know, Dennis, I'll just bet that I can put a hole through one of those cow's ears with one shot."

"You just get on outta here, Jack. You ain't gonna shoot no cow ears!"

"What's the matter with you? We used to do that back on dad's farm?"

"Yeah, I know we did but these are my cows!"

Agnes' sister, Rosella, was Doc's favorite aunt. He always remembered her saying, "There are no bad boys, some just do bad things." He used to chum around with Aunt Rosella's son, Mike, who was also a nimrod with the rifle. One morning, they were shooting blackbirds out in the far pasture pecking seeds out of the cow pies when Agnes called them in for lunch. Aunt Rosella always told them that they were not supposed to shoot colored birds, only blackbirds. So, during lunch, she asked, "Did you boys shoot any colored birds today?"

"Only a Red-Headed Woodpecker," said Mike.

Although the work consumed a major portion of Doc's life, he still had the time, the exuberance and more than likely the urge to get into a little trouble on his own now and again. Between his eighth and tenth years of age there were several incidents that would bring scolding and punishment in the Ed Casey manner that would make an indelible and lasting impression. A sterling example is when Doc and one of his brothers were wrestling in their upstairs bedroom and kicked the window, breaking glass.

It was in the middle of winter and for several days the wind would blow snow into the room. Each morning, before going to school, the boys had to shovel out the snow so that it would not melt and run down the steps. Each night they would shovel more out before going to bed under piles of quilts to keep warm. At times there would be six inches of snow on the floor beneath the window. After several frigid nights, Ed had the boys remove the window, have it repaired and pay for it themselves. They raised the money by trapping skunks and selling the pelts for $2.00 each.

For all their work, none of the Casey kids received an allowance. When the family would go into town on Saturday evenings, they might each get two-bits to spend as they wished. Edward would encourage, but not demand, that they save a little of their money for a rainy day. Sometimes they did.

Doc had a liking for the sweet, wet taste of watermelon, his or someone else's. Many a night, he and his buddies would sneak into the watermelon patches of neighboring farms and see how many they could get away with, even under threat of being peppered with buckshot. Everybody knew he was prime leader of the watermelon raids, but he was never actually caught in the act and was never identified in the dark of night.

There was no indoor plumbing so the family had to use the outdoor privy, an inconvenience disliked by Doc. He would sneak out on the porch at night to relieve himself after first making sure nobody would see him. One morning following a fresh snowfall his mom was shaking out bedding when she saw yellow spots dotting the otherwise fresh, white snow. She told Ed about it and that very night, he was waiting out of sight to see which of the kids was the culprit. Doc came sneaking out. As soon as the stream started, Ed shined a flashlight on, what Doc referred to as, his wee-wee. "Damn it, boy", Ed exclaimed, "next you'll want to bore a hole in the damn door!"

Christmas Eve was ritually celebrated at Mass. Christmas dinner was prepared and served in a traditional way, thanks to the blessings of fall harvests of vegetables and corn. The mouth-watering aroma of roasted turkey and baked ham set the family's stomachs to growling long before mealtime. Fresh baked bread or rolls liberally smeared with butter complimented the meal, making good soppin' for thick, rich, brown gravy flowing from mounds of mashed potatoes.

Mincemeat and pumpkin pies with their aromatic spices permeating the air, were consumed with groans of satisfaction at each bite. Some of the men would lay on the braided rug in the living room moaning, "My God, I won't be able to eat another bite until tomorrow." A lie, forgiven and forgotten when later in the evening, they would slap together a sandwich of two thick slices of white bread layered in the middle with whatever meat was left over.

Often, the only Christmas presents Doc and the other children received included an orange, an apple or banana and maybe a little candy. One day in the mid thirties, near Christmas Day, Doc was playing in the barn. He climbed up a big hay loft and there, on the very top, was a shiny red wagon. Jack, his brother, came in and when Doc told him about it, Jack said, "Aw, that's for our cousin, Bobby. Dad just hid it there for now." Doc was disappointed.

When Christmas morning came around, Doc went downstairs. Under the tree sat a red wagon. His name was on it! He learned that his dad had found the wagon in a junk yard. It was in a pretty sorry state but Ed repaired it and painted it with two coats of bright red paint just for Doc. It remained the most special Christmas in Doc's life and, more importantly, it was the first time that Doc realized his father loved him, as he loved all of his children although the words were never spoken.

The Casey house was not a big house. Space was at a premium with seven children of varied ages under one roof. Doc, for several years, slept in the same bed as his older sister, Virginia. Later on, he was getting a little embarrassed about this arrangement and said so to his dad. Ed replied, "Oh, Denny, it'll be all right!"

Doc came right back at him with, "But, dad, she is getting those bumps on her chest!" Ed moved him out that very night.

Saturday night was a special night in most farming communities, the night when everyone came to town to do their shopping, or sacrifice some coins to see a movie - a full feature, comedy and two cartoons. Folks would casually walk the streets and with other walkers discuss a broad range of subjects from health to politics. Many of them would end up at the local ice cream parlor to buy a double-dip real cream ice cream cone for a nickel. Others would spend time at the Scoreboard, a local bar. And there was, no doubt, a source for local "bootlegged" booze or "home brew" for those who wanted something a tad stronger than ice cream.

Ed sometimes shot a little pool and was at times referred to as a "Pool Shark" because of his skill at the game. "Shark" or not, the game provided him with a brief respite from farm work and worry. He and his family often stayed longer in town in the summertime. Eastern South Dakota summers, day or night, were never comfortable and air conditioning was a dream for the future.

Sometimes, there would be a dance, with a live band, usually a guitar, upright bass, and a drummer who would play the same repetitious beat bordering on boredom. On special evenings there would be a clarinet or a trumpet or both. Couples danced the two-step in pace with the music, more as a ritual than as a movement of pleasure and grace. Everybody took a turn on the floor, old farmers, young farmers, locals, embarrassed boys asking blushing girls, afraid that they would step on their toes. And they did.

Everyone was on equal footing, so to speak. The women wore fresh washed cotton dresses that had been washed and ironed so often the once bright flower prints had faded almost beyond recognition. Aroma of Eau de Cologne toilet water would blend, as the night lengthened, with the sweat smell from the energetic dancers. Sweating was a constant in their lives.

Many farmers wore their blue bib overalls over white starched shirts, open at the neck revealing frayed edges about the collar. A few wore neckties that were tied with a tight skinny knot pulled snugly on ill fitting collars. The face of each farmer was weather hammered and sun scorched with accented creases about the eyes from squinting down seemingly endless rows in dusty fields where they harrowed, raked, planted and hopefully harvested their much needed crops.

From their ears up a white crown of common sense, acquired knowledge that without wide brimmed work hats to protect their heads, the uncaring sun could and would cause them to fall victim to heat stroke. There was no time allowed in the work schedule of these tillers of sod for sickness, of any kind. Time lost could easily mean a lost crop. A lost crop, in these times, could mean a lost farm.

By 1941, folks were adjusting to the lifestyle of the Depression era, learning to get by with less but still needing more. One month before Doc Casey's tenth birthday, life on the farm and in Mitchell changed. December 7, 1941, the attack on Pearl Harbor. Only a few knew where Pearl Harbor was, fewer yet knew who the Japanese were. Everyone learned that life would never be the same.

When he turned ten, Doc was assigned, in addition to his other chores, the job of milking five cows, twice a day. He worked their teats with expert fingers that assured each swollen udder would yield every last drop of milk. He would then put the milk in clean and sterilized metal milk cans then place them in a water tank to keep the milk cool. There was no electricity on the farm to power the cooling boxes.

Doc continued to do all of these jobs throughout high school, gaining a measure of relief when Ed sold off the milk cows. He did not particularly like doing the work but it needed to be done. It was about this time in his life that Doc looked forward to the day that he could leave the farm, but not his family.

There were times in school when Doc just could not avoid fighting. He was a little guy, only weighing at most 90 pounds going into high school and usually got, in his words, the "shit" kicked out of him. About this time, his winning personality and easy ability to make friends was starting to blossom. He had formed a friendship with two good pals, Pesicka and Sullivan who watched out for Doc and would physically educate anyone who bullied him. The lessons were well learned. Later, both of his buddies would go to the state reform school for reasons long forgotten.

One fight Doc did not lose. He championed the cause of some girls at Notre Dame Academy who were being punched and shoved by male students. Doc was taught that a man, especially an Irishman, did not hit a woman, whatever the reason. He waded in with a display of vicious pugilistic skill which sent the assaulters scampering. It was, perhaps, the last time that he had to rely on physical prowess which gave way to his friendly demeanor, his Irish smile, his easy going attitude and the charming ability to diffuse negative situations.

When he was old enough for sports in school, Doc chose basketball but really did not get a chance to play. His father said there was too much work to do about the farm, and that came first. He would attend local games, cheering the Notre Dame team between mouthfuls of one of his favorite treats, popcorn. There were not many games in a season because at the time Catholic schools did not play against public school teams.

By now, Doc was earning his reputation as the most colorful member of the Casey family. He worked hard, played hard and loved an audience. He got along with all his siblings, establishing early on an alliance with his sister, Janice (Jan). They were, according to their older sister, Dee, "Two peas in a pod!" Their escapades would come to be almost as legendary as those of Doc and his brother Jack but in a somewhat different manner.

Rover was the farm dog with the responsibility of bringing the cows in from pasture. There was a small herd of milk cows and a Shetland pony in one pasture. Jack thought that Rover had something against the Shetland. Everytime he and Doc would tell him to go fetch the cows, Rover would cut out the Shetland then chase it full speed to the corral. His fun over, Rover would go back after the cows, bringing them in at a leisurely pace.

Jack and Doc had convinced some pals from town that Rover could understand spoken English and would do anything the boys asked their dog to do. When some of the boys would visit the farm, Jack or Doc would say to Rover, "Now, I want you to go out there and get the pony. Don't mess with those damn cows! Just bring in the pony. Go get 'em!" Rover performed as promised and the town boys thought the Caseys had the smartest dog in the country.

It was about this time that Doc made the acquaintance of Father Thomas James McPhillips. The two of them were kindred spirits, very much alike in many ways and formed a friendship would last a lifetime. Father Mac refers to the Casey family as, a saintly Irish mother, a stern and dominant father and loving brothers and sisters. Years later, several of Doc's own children would celebrate their first communion in the family room of their home in Rapid Valley in a Mass conducted by Father "Mac", complete with altar, vestments and the "holy" works.

Agnes, who was more active in looking at and buying real estate than her husband, had purchased another little farm where there was a lake, a couple of miles away from the 160 acre place. This was into World War II. Dee had gone off to college, Jerome enlisted in the Army and Ed Jr., was working for the government on highly classified projects. Hired help was impossible to get due to the war but Doc and Jan did a good job of handling the chores. By this time there were no more milk cows, just some beef cattle pastured on the farm where the Caseys lived or over at the "other place", as they called it.

In 1946, Ed bought his first tractor. Jan dubbed it, "A wonderful machine!" It greatly reduced the work time and work load. Jan liked to operate the tractor and enjoyed sprawling her legs over the sides to get suntanned. She would also handle the stacker while Doc built the hay stacks. They made a good team, although several times, Doc narrowly avoided being whacked off a stack by the erratic maneuvering of the machinery by Jan.

Doc took on some outside jobs to earn some spending money and, at the urging of Ed, set a little aside toward college. Doc and Jan were the only two left at home and had more available to them, including access to the 1928 Model A (which was decorated in the school colors). There was considerably more money available to them now that the older Casey kids were gone and times were economically better.

For some reason or another, Doc had driven their car to Omaha and he was pulled over by a patrolman who asked him for his driver's license, to which Doc replied, "License? We don't have any license to drive in South Dakota!" The Sheriff did not believe him, and Doc was put in the "hoosegow" for driving without a license. Later, checking Doc's story, the Sheriff learned that indeed a license was not required in South

Dakota and Doc was released. It was not until he was twenty years old that Doc had a driver's license.

One Fourth of July, when he was fifteen, Doc tried his hand at riding a bucking horse at a makeshift rodeo where the neighbors got together for a potluck picnic. He later recalled, "It was fun but I remember getting the shit kicked out of me! I never did it again. Probably because I got smarter!"

Doc had serious moments. Whenever he would get mad or had something to think out, he would leave the house and walk for hours about the Casey "Estate", as he used to call the farm. It was on one of these walks that he more than likely began laying out some semblance of a plan for his life after high school and away from Mitchell.

Sister Dee had gone off to the University of South Dakota to study Medical Technology, excelling in her studies. In the winter of 1949, she became violently ill. It was Typhoid Fever. Ed and Agnes were never so worried about any of their children as they were about Dee, hoping and praying continuously for her recovery. Everyone in the family had to take Typhoid shots. Dee slowly recovered and, with time, her health was restored. It was never determined from where she contacted the Typhoid Fever.

Father Thomas McPhillips regarding Doc's entry into high school, "He was the personification of the two names, Dennis Patrick. At home, the way he conducted himself with his father and mother, buffoonery with his brothers and sisters, was brought into school toward the Sisters, Priests and his classmates - the clown - never serious throughout life."

Doc was a good student in spite of his clowning and noted lack of seriousness. Part of his life was going in a more serious direction. It had been weighing on his mind for some time that he wanted to become a Catholic Priest. When he told his mother, she encouraged him, along with Father Mac, to pursue the Priesthood. He and Father Mac had many soul searching discussions about this major decision in Doc's life. Toward the end of high school, Doc was certain that he wanted to go to pre-seminary school. Upon graduation from Notre Dame Academy, he enrolled and left the next Fall for Carroll College in Helena, Montana.

Just before Doc graduated from Notre Dame, the school newspaper featured a photo of him with a large grin on his face, a grin that would become his trademark. In part, the accompanying story said, "Sure now, there was a wearin' o' the green on January 6, 1931 when the grinnin' Irish mug o' Dennis Patrick Casey first shone on this dismal earth. And, begorra, it's been shinin' just as bright these many years . . .!"

arroll was popular with several of the youth from the Mitchell. It had an excellent reputation in academics owing, in part, to the study regimen instilled by the Jesuits. Some of Doc's friends were enrolled there when he chose to go. Father Mac ferried some of the boys, including Doc, back and forth to Helena, wearing out three old Chevrolets. The first year, he was still encouraging Doc to consider the Priesthood. Doc was sincere in his thoughts of becoming a Catholic Priest but other influences reversed his decision. He would joke about it later by saying, "I changed my mind when I realized that I couldn't chase girls . . .!" But there was more than that going on inside the mind of Doc Casey.

After Doc left for Carroll, he was missed on the farm. Ed now had a hired hand. Jan did more than her share of the chores, thankful that Ed had sold the milk cows. The stocky herd of Aberdeen Angus took care of themselves for the most part. They were able to endure the harsh eastern South Dakota winters and required minimal tending or care as long as they had some hay and the water in the lake open enough for them to drink. Jan recalled that those days were dull without Doc.

During his Freshman year at Carroll, Doc was uncertain as to what he really wanted to do with his life. He wanted to join the Smoke Jumpers of the US Forest Service to fight forest fires. His dad was very much opposed to this. He did not exactly say that Doc could not join the Smoke Jumpers, full knowing that his son would probably do so to spite him. Ed Casey was smarter than that. Instead, he offered Doc a percentage on

CARROLL
COLLEGE

some land that produced cantaloupe. Doc agreed and the first year made some pretty good profit, all of which he wanted to spend, but Ed persuaded him to put some of the money in the bank. Doc did and was grateful for Ed's insistence because the next two years were poor years for the crop.

Doc took his wit and humor back with him to Carroll in the fall. He was instrumental in several practical jokes and campus escapades. Most memorable, perhaps, was when he led the charge on the girl's dormitory one night in popular panty raids. He was the first up the wall and into a window where he gained ground in the hallway and turned the fire hose on friend and foe. At this point in his never dull life, one must wonder at how often Doc Casey went to Confession and how long he would have stay in the booth unloading his happy burden.

Ed and Agnes were becoming concerned about the amount of money Doc was spending at Carroll. He was having a good time on his own and was probably a little more generous with the limited funds that his parents sent him than they felt he should be. In the spring of 1950 they had sent him $65.00 to come home on the bus or train. Doc had a friend in greater need of the money so he gave him $60.00 to help him out. Friends and associates often took advantage of Doc's generosity.

Doc had to hitchhike back to Mitchell. By the time he made it home, he had a badly infected foot. His toes and foot were about three times their normal size. Ed did not have very many kind words to say to Doc when he arrived home, bad foot or not. Doc went on antibiotics and soaked his foot five times a day for a week before the swelling subsided and the infection was stopped. The Casey home was pretty quiet and the air chilled during that week whenever Doc and his dad were together. Ed was concerned about the bum foot but was disgusted with Doc's charitable $60.00 act.

Later, at Carroll, Doc enrolled in business courses and mathematics. During school break one fall he was out in the Quonset hut stacking bales of hay. The mail had come, one letter from Carroll, a copy of Doc's grade reports for the semester. Ed always read these reports to see how his boy was doing. After reading the latest reports, he walked out to the Quonset and asked Doc, "What's this business, math and business accounting stuff? Going to be a businessman and sit on your ass for the rest of your life?"

"No, I think I've changed my mind again. What I want to do is go to Creighton in Omaha and take up pre-dental." said Doc.

"Well, do whatever you want, Dennis. Just make up your mind."

Dennis' mind was made up. After three years at Carroll College, he applied to dental school. In August 1951, Doc began his studies. Here, he found his niche in the professional and business world. It was just the beginning in the saga of Dennis Patrick Casey, one of satisfaction, disappointments and fulfillment. It was accomplished without sacrificing

his outlook, his friendliness, and his Irish sense of humor always
highlighted by his Irish smile.

When Doc Casey started his dental education in the fall of 1951, there were forty-six in the class, several more than the standard class. It was the time of the Korean Police Action. There was a shortage of dentists for the military services. Creighton was encouraged by the Government to increase the number of students with the assurance that if they kept their grade averages high, they would be deferred from the draft until such time as they qualified and graduated with a DDS.

Somewhere along the way from Mitchell to Creighton, Doc had acquired some sense of responsibility and maturity in his life and knew damn good and well that if he was to be a dentist, he had to buckle down. He and his classmates were not, however, prepared for the discipline awaiting them each and every day in class and lab.

With time, those who acquired strong study habits managed to keep up with the mumbo-jumbo numbers, terminology, names of instruments and compounds. Their instructors funneled through their ears a seemingly alien language. Their addled brains hoped to absorb and translate all of this knowledge into useful

CREIGHTON CLASS OF '55

practice. If they did not let down their mental guard or miss a night of reading, researching and hours of examining each other's teeth and gums, and learning to see things backwards in a mirror no larger than a Buffalo Nickel, there was a good chance that they would one day be dentists.

Doc and his comrades of the hopeful Class of 1955 sometimes must have wondered what they were doing there and if the four years ahead of them would, rather than creating dentists, leave them mindless, exhausted shells of once strong and intelligent young men.

Doc's playful, childlike Irish self, temporarily subdued by the rigors of study, emerged even stronger after awhile. Not even the harsh discipline of the Jesuit persuasion could keep the likes of the namesake of St. Patrick, himself, subdued forever. His infectious humor, often fueled by the quaffing of fermented beverages, flowed happily into the lives of his classmates and all whom he met thereafter. Doc was drinking and smoking considerably more than when he was in Mitchell or even at Carroll.

The Class of '55 remembered Doc fondly and eagerly shared their stories.

Kenneth A. Harman, DDS, had this to say:

"Casey (we always called him Casey, never Dennis) was a unique, one of a kind guy. He kept the class from getting dull or taking themselves too seriously. But, you sensed that underneath there was a serious, solid character who would do well at dentistry or any other endeavor. He had a multitude of friends of course, and left the world a better place for having been there.

"One day my wife came home laughing from the clinic where Casey and another classmate had just treated the patients and other "prospective" dentists to a squirt gun fight while the instructors were out of the room. They were all entertained for the afternoon.

"We all remember him fondly and believe that as Cardinal Newman said, May He protect us all day long 'till the shades lengthen and the evening falls and the busy world is hushed, the furor of life is over and our work is done. Then in His mercy, may He give us safe lodging and holy rest and peace at the last."

"Casey has surely been granted a safe lodging and holy rest."

Allen W. Brown, DDS, adds:

"I was a classmate of Dennis in the class of 1955. I happened to have been very fortunate because in that class our seating arrangements were alphabetical and with a name like Brown, I had the privilege of sitting next to Casey for four years of dental school, in the front row, of course.

"When you sat next to Dennis there were very few dull moments. It did not matter how tough or complex things might be in class, Dennis always had a quip, joke or 'bit of wisdom' that may strike you later that day, week or month. Dennis certainly helped me, and I am sure many of my classmates, make it through our training with many more smiles and 'bits of wisdom' that we will remember the rest of our lives.

"After graduation, I only had the opportunity to see Dennis one more time. Approximately ten years after graduation, my family and myself took a trip through the Dakotas. While traveling through Rapid City, I called Dennis and met him for lunch. The short lunch extended to a much longer lunch with many laughs and memories. While we were in the restaurant it was amazing how many people stopped by to say hello to Dennis. This was the last time that I had the privilege of his presence.

"I do not know why, but when I learned of Casey's death, it hit me as hard as the death of one of my own family members. After much thought, I realized that the reason I was so upset was that after sitting next to Dennis for four years, Dennis was a member of 'my family.'

"Dennis will always be remembered and have a spot in my heart. I am sure he has a smile on his face and thinking of his next 'bit of wisdom' to pass on. Goodbye, Dennis, you are and will be missed, but you will always be remembered . . ."

Vince Licari, DDS, stated:

"Many of our classmates were WW II Veterans and were married, so didn't have as much contact in school with the younger single students. However, as the years passed, the gap in our relationships narrowed and we became a very close, cohesive class. Our five year interval reunions became a highlight of our friendships, and of course Dennis became a huge contributor to our festivities.

"Dennis and my wife Norma became great friends, mostly because of his bizarre sense of humor and wit. They were hale and hearty friends. He hosted us at a dental meeting in Rapid City about 1965, and we brought six of our staff with us. After three days with Dennis and his Irish antics, they asked, 'How did you guys ever graduate?'

"On or about our 35th class reunion, most of the out of town guests were holed up at the Embassy Suites on the west end of Omaha. The night of our class dinner party, Dennis shows up in his cowboy regalia and proceeded to entertain all of us. The highlight of his tale was when he told us he came to Omaha in an 18-wheeler in which he delivered cattle to the stockyards. What he didn't tell us was that the rig and cattle were parked in the Embassy parking lot - a typical Casey 'live it up, aw, what the heck, whose going to find out' laugh. He was one of a kind and I hope he and Norma are having fun up there. . ."

Les Pitman, DDS, said:

"Dennis and Bob Manion roomed together. They were close friends. Dennis told me that he and Bob had gone out for a little liquid refreshment one evening and ended up at an American Legion or VFW

Post. If I recall correctly, it was located around 15th and Cass and was an old house converted to club use. They were getting ready to leave and had gone to use the men's room. Now this room was equipped with a linen towel machine that dispensed a clean segment from one roller as it wound the soiled section onto another roller. I don't remember if Dennis said the machine was broken or whether he and Manion had tried to adjust it. At any rate, they had both rolls of towel out of the machine. Dennis proceeded to wrap Bob up like a mummy with toweling near the foyer. With Bob thoroughly mummy-wrapped, Casey started to pull on the loose end and converted Manion into a spinning top and spun him right through the plate glass window of the front door. They both left immediately, of course, and Bob was unscathed!

"My favorite Casey story is about Dennis in the prosthetic department. At Creighton there was no shortage of denture patients. One day, a nice gentleman came to us in need of full upper and lower dentures. He had just recently arrived from Italy and knew no English. There were several students of Italian extraction in our class: Cutuli, Gentile, D'Angelo, Marenco, Pieri, plus a few others who probably knew some Italian but who did they assign the patient to? None other than that famous Italian dentist, Dennis Casey! Casey probably only knew three acceptable words in Italian - pizza, spaghetti and macaroni - all the rest were cuss words.

"Dennis and his patient hit it off famously and conversed with all sorts of sign language and gestures. . . students were required to take dental impressions in plaster of Paris which is mixed to a consistency of thick pea soup, loaded into an impression tray, placed in the patient's mouth and seated. There is always an excess in the tray and it kind of squishes out over the edge of the tray. The plaster sets very quickly and upon setting is like stone.

"Casey's patient also possessed a big, bushy 'Groucho Marx' mustache. Casey mixed the plaster, loaded the tray, placed it in the patient's mouth and seated it. The plaster worked out of the tray and into the patient's mustache and set up immediately. Under the best of conditions, these impressions were tough to remove but here the plaster and tray are also locked into a mustache! Dennis would try to remove the tray and the patient would begin to squirm as his mustache was pulled! After much gesticulating, squirming and pulling, Dennis was finally triumphant and I congratulated him on being the first dental student to successfully get an impression of a mustache."

Robert J. "Bob" Manion, DDS, said:

"Dennis is a double personification of the word character. He had an abundance of it. He certainly was one.

"Our time in school wasn't without some extra curricular hi-jinks and Dennis was never outdone in this department. Although never destructive or cruel, if anyone accused, his reply was, 'When shame comes my way, I admits it!'

"As 'best man' at our wedding and Godfather to our oldest child, Dennis has always been a very close friend. When I realize that not even he could dodge the grim reaper, it gives me pause and sadly reminds me of my own mortality.

"A few years ago, on our way to Albuquerque, we stopped in Rapid City and called Dennis. To my surprise, he was in the hospital. We visited him and I was taken aback. He looked tough, and the usual bright look in his eyes was gone. We went to Albuquerque and came home. I was reluctant to call Dennis, fearing what I would hear.

"After putting it off a week or so, I called the house. Dennis answered and sounded good. He had been to a hospital in Denver, and with some new tech and medicine, he was doing better. I told him the last time I visited him in the hospital, and looked into his eyes, it didn't look good.

"'Hell', he replied with the old Casey bravado, 'you shoulda seen it from my side!'"

"I spoke to Dennis later when he was in assisted living. He wasn't able to talk much. His condition had worsened. In the last silent moments, before I said so long to my old friend, I had a quick flashback to my wedding day when he was, and still is, the 'best man' ."

When Doc was into his second year at Creighton, his sister Jan, was enrolled in the nursing school. Life on Creighton campus would never be the same. Their sister, Dee, was, as Jan would say, "Lucky enough to be living in Omaha at the time", and she probably thought that was a little more responsibility for the family than she cared to carry because Doc and Jan were always into some kind of trouble.

It was but a matter of time before the development of a brother and sister dating service. Jan kept Doc supplied with dates as needed and Doc did likewise for her. There Doc had acquired a taste for and liking of vodka, sometimes as a martini, sometimes not, the only difference being an olive. At the same time, his smoking dramatically increased, perhaps as a result of the pressure of continuing studies or the socializing or perhaps both. Or maybe he just enjoyed smoking.

The Class of 1955 worked, studied and played together. The friendships that were formed remain just as solid today. When they finally graduated, many were issued military orders, commissioned officers in the various

SOCIAL LIFE AT CREIGHTON

military branches of service. They went their separate ways to become successful in private practice, raising families and serving their chosen communities.

Doc had attended his last two years at Creighton on an ROTC scholarship and now was obligated to serve two years of active duty. His first year as a dentist was served in the most unlikely of places, Pickstown, South Dakota, where the Corps of Engineers was constructing Fort Randall Dam, the town he would always refer to as the "Best little town by a damsite!"

The Corps of Engineers hospital at Pickstown was a small thirty-two bed medical facility with one small office for dental needs. When Doc showed up for the job, a gangly young Irishman, confident and smiling, he had no way of knowing that the fates guiding him to this little spot on the Missouri River would result in a major happening in his life.

Eugene and Bridget Flynn supervised the medical facility. The moment they met Doc, they took an immediate liking to him. From that day on, "Uncle" Eugene and "Aunt" Bridget took him under the generous spread of their wings. There was also a third member of their family, Bridget's brother, Patrick Kenny, who would quickly ally himself with the new dentist.

Patrick Kenny had secured a job on the dam construction through Eugene and Bridget who were more or less looking out for his welfare. Patrick emigrated from Ireland to New York some years before, where he worked along with some of his kin as a bartender. He was known to "tip a few" now and again, if not more than a few, and in the long run, the family felt that the clean air of the west and the guidance of the Flynns would wean good old Patrick at least partially from the drink.

Dennis Patrick Casey met his ilk in the person of one Patrick Kenny. The two of them would share some harrowing times together during their time off. There were frequent trips to Lake Andes and other nearby towns. Stories of the fun loving duo's capacity for drinking and antics bordered on legendary. The only requirement necessitating their visits to these

PICKSTOWN AND PAULINE

eastern South Dakota towns was that there be a bar, and two or more would do nicely, thank you! It was in the company of Patrick, the 100% Irishman from 'over there', that the complete Irish came out in Doc to be refined and ripened as the years went on.

Doc's fondness for a dram or two was equaled by his enjoyment of Irish music. He loved the Clancy Brothers (who he had the good fortune to later see "live" in Greenwich Village, New York). He had a fair voice himself. Everytime Bridget would walk in the hallway past the dentist's office, Doc would break into, "It's A Long Way To Tipperary" with "the" grin on his mug and the voice of an angel, if but with one wing. He endeared himself to the family Flynn and, of course, his new mate from the "old sod", Patrick.

The Flynns had a visitor from California that summer, Bridget's niece, Pauline Foley. Pauline was born in New York. Her family moved to California in 1942. She was presently attending the nursing school at Mount Saint Mary's College in Los Angeles, and spent her summers with her Uncle Eugene and Aunt Bridget, working in the hospital. Pauline was an apt student, and the experience was priceless. She was not, however, prepared for one new experience. She was about to meet the new dentist in town.

The California girl and the wild-eyed Irishman became fast friends from their first meeting. They dated a few times and shared a lot of time with Eugene and Bridget, and sometimes Patrick. Doc and Patrick of course were still doing their spare time jaunts away from Pickstown. Doc was smitten from the start, but he did not want to get involved on a serious level and certainly was not looking for a long term relationship.

The defining date was when he asked Pauline out and the entire family went along, Eugene, Bridget and Patrick. They all went in Patrick's big Cadillac to a nearby bar. Under ordinary circumstances, this could have be construed as the beginning of a courtship. Doc was nervous but hid it well. All in all, it was a fun evening, enjoyed by everyone. On the drive home, during a lull in conversation, Patrick asks, "Dennis, how'd you like to be buried with our people?"

"What kind of people am I with?" thought Doc. He was in his mid twenties, newly graduated from dental school with a full life ahead of him and this clan of Irish folk were already planning his funeral? Obviously, the final stamp of approval had been set upon the likes of Dennis Patrick Casey. What was he to do? When the time came for Pauline to return to California, he knew, for certain that he would have to see her again.

That same year, construction on Fort Randall Dam was winding down. The job site was closed, leaving only a skeleton crew for inspections and clean up. Eugene and Bridget, along with Patrick, went upriver to Pierre, South Dakota where another Corps dam, Oahe, was being constructed and a medical facility was in operation. Doc went along until he would be reassigned to a permanent Air Force job.

Doc had a friend, Basil Haas, a dentist, who also was a member of the Class of '55. Basil was probably the closest friend that Doc had at the time. During their time together at Creighton they would sometimes share dreams. Part of the dreams was a plan that they would one day become partners in their own clinic. Eugene and Aunt Bridget could see the chemistry between the two young men at once. Doc and Basil became part of the family, often eating meals with the Flynns or just visiting together.

Doc and Basil formed a partnership and opened a dental office in Pierre. Doc's call up came from the US Air Force but a short time later. In 1956, Dr. Casey was commissioned as Captain Casey. After training and orientation, he was assigned to Guam. His partner would continue their practice until such time as Doc would return and they could again work together.

Doc's tour of duty at Anderson Air Force Base on Guam went well, thanks in part to his friendship with his dental assistant, Charlie Manley. They were kindred spirits. Both of them were endowed with a sense of humor that, at times, bordered on bizarre. Whenever the mood hit, they would do a "Frick and Frack" routine, totally spontaneous and without rehearsal, that would shake the very foundations of military order.

In one of their "skits", Doc would have a patient in the chair. After the preliminary examination, he would instruct Charlie to prepare the injection for numbing the area to be worked upon. Charlie would leave the room and return holding a 50cc "monster" size syringe full of water which he would be squirting in the air, assuring that the patient could see the whole thing. The results ranged from hilarious to anxious, depending upon who was in the chair at the time. The dental clinic at Anderson was never dull thanks to Doc and Charlie.

Doc and Charlie did a lot of socializing together. When asked if Doc did much smoking and drinking on Guam, Charlie replied, "Well, if you could buy cigarettes for twelve cents a pack and good grade scotch for a buck-fifty, what would you do?" And they did, as there was not a whole lot of anything else to do.

Guam had it's good moments but Doc was already looking forward to the day he could return to South Dakota. He enjoyed his brief stint with the Air Force but it did not take him long to decide that it was not where he wanted to spend his dental career. His frequent thoughts of Pauline did not help matters either. Her letters helped to partly ease his homesickness. Work, Charlie and "happy hour" filled in the rest. He was counting the days until his tour over, marking x's on a calendar with each passing day.

Doc had not been on Guam a year when he was called into the Unit Commander's office and informed that Father McPhillips had sent a message, through the Red Cross. Basil Haas had been killed in an automobile accident in Pierre. He was driving home one evening and lost control of his car. The car skidded off of the road and hit a big Elm tree, head on, killing Basil instantly. It was believed that Doc's best friend had

GUAM

fallen asleep at the wheel. The news devastated Doc. He was given leave to return to Pierre for Basil's funeral, and to close their office, referring patients to other dentists.

It was not a pleasant flight home. Upon boarding the first commercial flight, Doc took solace in vodka until the final leg on a "puddle jumper" propeller job had touched down at the Pierre airport where he was met by his friend and mentor, Father Mac. "Might know," Father Mac would later remark, "Dennis came fortified with five-fifths minus one which he claimed to have shared with the airline stewardesses."

It was summer. As she had done the summer before, Pauline Foley, student nurse from California, was visiting her Uncle Eugene and Aunt Bridget who were still with the Corps medical facility in Pierre. One evening, Eugene, Bridget and Pauline were sitting in Eugene's car outside the "Snake Pit", a bar in Fort Pierre, across the river, watching people walk in and stagger out. This was a popular pastime in a town that did not offer much in the way of "family" entertainment, and provided a laugh now and again at the expense of some poor drunk who could not hit his butt with both hands.

Pauline was sitting in the rear seat of the car, her hair done up in rollers. It was a warm, muggy evening and the rear windows were rolled down. She was startled by a sharp rap on the roof of the car and turned her head to the right to see the grinning face of Doc. "War is hell!" said Doc. That is all, just, "War is hell!". Pauline felt the rush of two emotions simultaneously. First, she was blushingly embarrassed that she was seen with the rollers in her hair. Second, she felt a surge of happiness at seeing the dentist guy she had met the summer before. Thus began the serious courtship of Dennis Patrick Casey and Pauline Foley.

Doc and Pauline talked about his eventual separation from the military and his plans to return to South Dakota. They both knew that they wanted to see each other and be with each other again. Doc asked her if she would consider moving closer, to South Dakota when he returned. He thought that he wanted to marry Pauline but was not sure. Up to now, they had been communicating mostly by phone and letters, and a nervous Doc thought that perhaps they should get to know each other better. Before Doc returned to duty on Guam, Pauline had agreed.

Doc had an itch on both feet to see some of the world before going home. He was being reassigned stateside to Ellsworth Air Force Base in Rapid City for separation. He applied for a 30 day furlough which was approved. He trekked to the Philippines, Hong Kong, Bangkok and on to New Delhi where he joined up with another world traveler. He told the story many times about meeting his traveling companion but never said who he was. The two of them wandered on to Italy then hitchhiked north to Hamburg, Germany visiting the notorious Herbert Strasse and drank more than one beer in the Zillertahl, the renowned music and beer hall auf der RepperBahn.

Bremerhaven, a short distance from Hamburg was their next stop and the end of the hitchhiking. Doc had ordered a VW Beetle, while yet on Guam, to be picked up in Bremerhaven, Germany. From there, the two traveling companions drove all over Europe to and through Austria, Switzerland, Denmark, Sweden and Norway before Doc reluctantly decided that it was time to return to South Dakota, where he was assigned to Ellsworth Air Force Base.

It would be here that Doc would settle down, at least geographically. The VW was shipped to New York where it was picked up later and driven back to South Dakota where it was used for several years including transportation for Kevin, the eldest Casey son, back and forth to high school. As for exact details of the world tour? There was no written or oral record. There were color slides now not to be found. The reader is justified to let imagination flow freely to create their own story, having read thus far about the exploits of the Leprechaun cleverly disguised as a dentist.

Casey Family Photo Album

Top Left: Ed Casey, Top Right: Maurice Casey,
Bottom Left: Dennis Casey, Bottom Right: Jack Casey

Jan and "Doc" Casey on Family Farm

Above:
The Ed Casey family picnicking in the shelter of their tree strip on the farm which they had once planned to abandon. The water-melons were raised on parts of the farm where previously it had been impossible to raise anything.

Right:
"Doc" at Creighton College

The Casey's - Mitchell, SD

Counterclockwise from bottom left:
Ed, Agnes, Dee, Virginia, Jan, Jerry, "Doc", Jack, Ed Jr.

Pauline, "Doc" & Jan – Pickstown, SD

Pauline and "Doc's" Wedding Day

That Irish Grin

"Doc" contemplating fence

Wolf
licking
"Doc",
Alpha Male

"Doc" feeding climbing bear cub

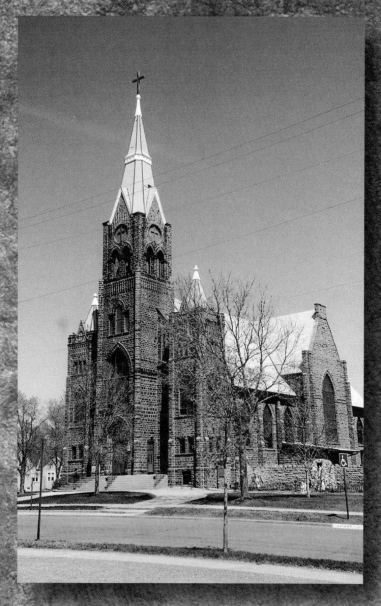

Holy Family Church - Mitchell, SD

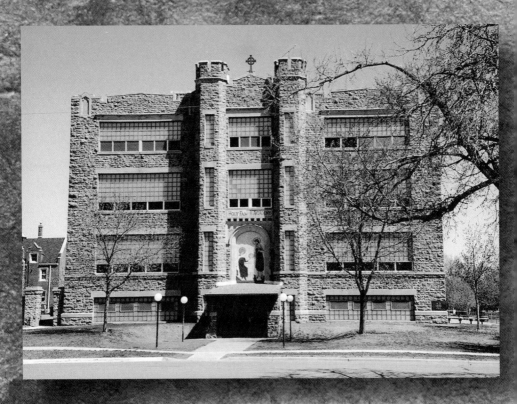

Notre Dame High School - Mitchell, SD

"Doc" vacationing in Hawaii

The Kenny Famly–
Pauline's kin in Ballygar, Ireland

Bearly enough room for all

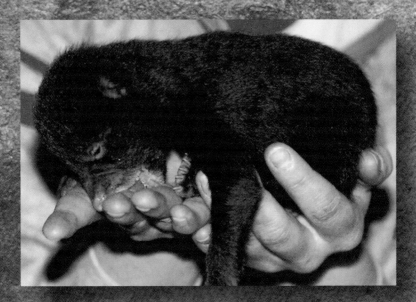

Newborn black bear

The Casey's - L to R: Sean, Mike, Brendan,
Kevin, Pauline, "Doc", Shannon, John, Dennis

After separation from the Air Force, Doc decided to remain in Rapid City as a dentist. He moved in with Dr. Al Olmacher in the beginning, but being the independent cuss he was, Doc left Olmacher to open his own practice. He bought a corner lot on Jackson Boulevard and Sheridan Lake Road. This was also beginning of his speculating and buying land, one parcel at a time, in the Black Hills.

Doc had a one story brown brick building with a basement built on the lot. He did a majority of the work himself on the inside. Father Mac came to visit during this time and was recruited to lend a hand. He was amazed and amused at Doc's apparent disregard for plaster and paint dripping from the ceiling onto his luggage and took it upon himself to periodically shift the bags out of harm's way. The Dennis P. Casey, DDS, Dental Office was finished in 1959 and Dr. Casey actively practiced there until 1991.

Gordon K. Magnusson, DDS , a longtime friend and colleague of Doc's, shared several personal observations:

"First thing that I must say about Dennis is that there was no one else just like him. He was truly a 'character' who, in my opinion, played a role in life far better than most of us in some ways, and like all the rest of us, had areas in which he would himself despair regarding his failure to 'do it correctly!'.

"He was a man whose personality was faceted and who possessed an inner intensity that served to magnify his good points . . . and his bad points beyond the verbiage accepted by most of us as deviations from the so called

RAPID CITY AND BEYOND

'normal!'. Dennis Casey had a heart as big as the Great Outdoors, was a kind, generous, helpful man who was much loved by many people. He was very much a free spirit!

"When he built a building to house his own equipment and practice at the corner of Jackson Boulevard and Sheridan Lake Road, he followed suit, taking into his office in following years several young graduates out of dental college who appreciated and needed the help of an older dentist to get started in their own careers.

"When one of those young men 'stiffed' Dennis by leaving his office to go into another one with several other dentists while leaving a large accumulation of unpaid rent to Dennis behind, I heard about it from someone else but had never heard a word about it from Dennis. He was not the sort of man to disparage others."

In the meantime, Pauline completed her nurse's training and graduated in 1957 then worked for awhile as a public health nurse with the Los Angeles County Health Department in the Watts District. In August 1958, with the blessings of her family, she moved to Rapid City. She had a small apartment at the Truax Apartments and was employed at the Pennington County Health Department in Rapid City. The dentist and the nurse were together until autumn waned into winter, time enough to indeed know each other better. Pauline told Doc that she was planning to fly home to California to be with her parents at Christmastime and it was then that Doc realized he wanted his friend to also share life with him as his wife.

Doc moved fast, as time was short. He had a friend from the Class of 1955 send him a diamond for a ring. Once the ring was made, shortly before Pauline was to leave, a nervous Doc went to her apartment. He proposed. She accepted and departed for California to make wedding plans. It was a match of opposites with the promising future of compassion, compromise, commitment and conflict. But what a future it would be.

Once the traditional arrangements were made, a date was agreed upon. The wedding would be in Compton, California on June 20, 1959, plenty of time to prepare, for everyone except of course for Doc. He called upon God to go with him to California and be at his side to shore up his courage but God was busy so he sent one Father Thomas James McPhillips in His stead. Father Mac, always the friend through thick and thin, had a large task before him before this wedding was completed.

Doc reserved two seats on a Western Airlines flight to California. Father Mac arrived in Rapid City the day before they departed and stayed overnight in the nondescript yet comfortable living area in the dental office of Doc Casey. Recalling the time, Father Mac said, "I believe

Dennis was using me as some sort of wedding gift - such a Romeo! I was to pack (after cleaning the plaster and paint off the luggage) while Dennis was still drilling and filling teeth up above. What a mess! No pants, worn out skivvies, shortage of socks.

"Enroute to the airport, we made the mistake of stopping at the Alex Johnson bar for a quick one or two. I had to remind Dennis that it was plane time. Our flight was already on the runway when we arrived at the airport but they called the plane back to pick us up. Once on the plane, after an inflight drink, Dennis, out of the blue, said, 'Now I remember where I left that damn convertible! At my cabin site in Hill City!' I didn't understand and said nothing. However, at the first stop, he deplaned and called someone to pick up the car.

"When our plane landed, I was instructed to let him off first to meet Pauline. I was to ignore them as I walked past, to no avail. Pauline screamed, 'Dennis, there's Father Mac!'. Caught. Dennis admitted that I was his wedding gift."

Before the wedding, Father Mac pulled Doc and Pauline aside and told them that if they had anything to talk about, do it now. Pauline came right out and asked Doc, "Have you ever been with other women?"

"I'm an average 29 year old man . . . what about that Kinsey Report?"

"It says an average of five to six partners before marriage."

"Well, Pauline, I consider one average."

Father Mac once again assumed the role of Dennis Patrick Casey's guardian angel when he bought some new undershorts and loaned him a pair of black socks for the wedding. It was a grand wedding and, in spite of his nervousness and being "scared spitless", Doc managed to stammer out "I do", and he did, and Pauline did. They were married.

After the reception, the newlyweds departed on their honeymoon before returning to Rapid City. First, they drove up to northern California where they spent a wonderful time enjoying the beauty of the coast for several days before driving to Reno, Nevada. After a couple of days in Reno, Doc and Pauline determined that they had enough for a nice dinner and hotel then back to South Dakota.

They drove back via Montana for a visit at Carroll College to meet Doc's mentor and friend, Ray Hunthausen. Ray was not there at the time. His younger brother, Art, was the assistant dean and they all had a nice visit, after which Doc gave Pauline a tour of the campus. It was obvious to Pauline that Doc was very proud of his alma mater.

Their first home in Rapid was the "living" area of the dental office on Jackson and Sheridan Lake Road. The morning after returning from their honeymoon, Pauline cooked her first meal, bacon and eggs, both, according to Doc, "very crisp!". Pauline set about sanitizing, rearranging and knick-knacking their temporary home that took up two-thirds of the building, kitchen, living room, bathroom, three bedrooms and a washer and dryer in the unfinished basement. This would be home until 1961 when they moved to the old Walt Hall ranch in Rapid Valley, east of Rapid City, on 45 acres of fertile land. Over the years, they added on, several times.

Gordon Magnusson shares some more thoughts on Doc:

"Dennis joined our local Dental Society and regularly attended the meetings. I was fascinated by the way he would sit back without comment for a great share of a meeting and finally, when the topic of discussion among his colleagues seemed to be completely entangled, rise to his feet and give a clear-cut, thoughtful analysis of the situation together with a logical and appropriate course of action!

"He loved to visit with his patients and anyone else who would drop into the office, and often had a waiting room full of people to see while he was visiting with someone and enjoying it so much that his schedule of appointments would go unattended."

As a dentist, Dr. Casey did his best to put his patients at ease. Often, he would give a preliminary course to whoever was sitting in the chair before beginning the actual exam and whatever treatment was needed. He would begin with individual instruments, explaining their purpose - the mirror, explorer, probe and types of forceps and their uses from exams to extraction's, continuing if needed with how any work, fillings etc., would be done and what it entailed from the injection of numbing anesthetics to fillings of their molars, bicuspids, cuspids or incisors with amalgam or composite compounds. A comfortable patient is a happy patient.

On one occasion, Doc had a small boy in the chair and had just finished a filling. He stood back, while his assistant was removing the bib from the boy, "Say, you may not be able to eat any hard candy for awhile!" It was lunchtime. The waiting room was devoid of patients. What did Doc do? He took both the boy and his mother to McDonald's for a burger, fries and chocolate malt. Young people had a special place in Doc Casey's heart. This was repeatedly demonstrated. He echoed an old Irish saying, "God watches out for drunk Irishmen and small children." He did, and He does.

Just since his dental days on Guam, Doc was amazed at the improvements, new techniques and updating of instruments in the dental field. He kept current, reading professional journals and papers and visiting with representatives of various companies that manufactured and marketed equipment, instruments and all products associated with the trade, from curettes to syringes, almagams to Xylocaine. Modern dentistry was constantly changing for the better for both dentist and patient.

A patient of almost thirty years had heard that a biography of Doc was in the works and that stories were being solicited and offered one of many. She was sitting in the waiting room for her appointment, waiting and waiting. It was the first appointment of the day. Doc was late but finally came sweeping through the door, "I sure am sorry I'm late but you see, I'm married to a New York girl, and the cow needed milking, and she doesn't know how to milk 'em nor does she have any desire to. So, I reckon that's my job and I just had to milk 'em or they'd utterly burst their udders!". How could anyone be upset with his being late after a story like that?

Pauline gave birth to their first child, a big baby boy, David, on May 17, 1960. It was a complicated breech delivery. David's brain was deprived of oxygen for eighteen minutes, and he died shortly after birth, the same day. Pauline was emotionally and physically drained, confined to her hospital bed. Doc was to see to the preparations for burial. David's death was a painful experience for Doc, a burden that he would carry for the rest of his life.

Forty years later, Doc's only daughter, Shannon, had bought a book, "A Father's Legacy", that had one question on each page. When Doc was home during hospice care, November 1998 to March 1999, each member of the family took turns sitting with him and would ask a question or two from the book. They would write down Doc's response.

One question: "When you were a new father, what was your greatest fear? Your greatest joy?"

Doc thought a moment before answering. "We don't count the one that died, right? The greatest fear was that when our son died, and the oxygen was cut off to his brain that he would be mentally deficient all his life. So, when he died, I didn't know whether to feel good or bad. That is a hell of a thing to say but it is true . . . Greatest joy, all the rest of you kids. All the rest of you came along good!"

Pauline and Doc enjoyed each other and the company of their many friends. The favorite nightspot during their first years of their marriage was the Esquire Club. Saturday nights at the Esquire were a "must do". The club was spacious and the atmosphere informal. The steaks were juicy. The drinks were sufficiently strong, and there was always a band. Along with some of their best friends, the Casey's did their fair share of socializing and dancing.

Doc was still keeping an eye out for good land investments. He knew one day there would be a family and he wanted, more than anything, to assure that his family would have a secure future. As with any true Irishman, Doc, as a boy, always believed that somewhere at the end of a rainbow, the Leprechauns had hidden a pot filled with gold, just waiting for the lucky soul who searched the longest and hardest and possessed the guile to outsmart these devious little legendary Irish tricksters. He thought that there could indeed be a pot at the end of a rainbow but it was an empty pot to be filled with one shiny coin at a time, coins earned by the sweat of the brow, prudent investing and regular savings. He never stopped believing in Leprechauns, only in the blarney about pots already full of gold.

"Y ou want to start a what?", asked a startled John Vucurevich. Doc Casey repeated his statement, "I want to start a wildlife park where folks can drive through in the comfort of their cars and be able to see animals in the wild, roamin' free, no cages, no bars." He could not understand Vucurevich's reaction. It seemed like a perfectly workable plan to him. "The whole idea came to me like a bolt of lightning when Pauline and the kids and I were driving through Yellowstone Park last year." It was July 1971. Doc had already mentioned his idea to Pauline and she did not have too many questions. The kids thought that it was just great.

John was one of Doc's patients and the two had become good friends. Both family men. Both visionaries, the only difference being that John was a tad more conservative and practical than Doc. Both were boosters of Catholic education and supporters of the St. Martin's school west of Rapid City. Their differences showed here also.

One year, St. Martin's was having trouble getting enrollments and was trying several approaches to the problem. Doc suggested to John, "Well, why don't we just call it a Christian school?".

"No", John came back, "When you say Catholic, people know what you're talking about. When you say Christian, they're not sure . . .!"

Doc would describe John Vucurevich as one of the most interesting people that he had ever met and a very honest man who did not flaunt his wealth. John repeatedly said that

BEAR COUNTRY USA

he and Doc were very good friends. Perhaps that is why the banker who owned Rushmore State Bank at the time was sitting beside his friend in the Alex Johnson Hotel bar listening to a wild idea about wildlife.

Doc had long ago purchased approximately 400 acres on top of Highway 16 south of Rapid City on the way to Mount Rushmore where he had a fine herd of registered Angus cattle. Part of this acreage would be the location of the wildlife park. John asked many questions, the standard ones regarding collateral mostly. All Doc had was his building on Jackson Boulevard. After several more visits with John and the bank and offering up his dental office for collateral plus some land, Doc walked away with a hefty check, generous enough to get him started.

Fences were the first thing to build, strong fences, high fences that would contain bears and wolves and whatever other critters would eventually take up residence at the newest attraction in the Black Hills of South Dakota, Bear Country USA. It was hard work. Each post was challenged by rocks that were there long before fence posts. The project would be unavoidably put temporarily on hold because of the great Rapid City flood in June 1972. All of the fence workers left to drive debris trucks after the flood.

Father Don Murray at Sky Ranch got wind of the dilemma. He and Doc were always good friends. Father Murray sent eight or ten of his resident boys to Bear Country to complete the fencing. They camped on the premises and had one or two young seminarians as their custodians, counselors and work supervisors. They all did a great job.

Fence completed. Only one little detail left. Animals! The first acquisition was one wolf, eleven Black Bears from Minnesota and three Bison (buffalo to Westerners). With time, animals were purchased from zoos and animal ranches in the USA and Canada. From day one, the animals from the wild that Bear Country would accept would have to come from Game, Fish and Parks Departments of other states. The wild bear cubs were usually found after a mother bear was killed by a car accident or perhaps killed by poachers. Most Game and Fish Departments do not, as a rule, have the facilities to hand raise small cubs and Bear Country was always happy to receive them.

These creatures had to be fed and watered of course, and bears had to have deep, dark dens in which to hibernate and, hopefully, have their cubs. There was also the matter of health inspections and approval by USDA, state and local authorities before the animals could be purchased and released at Bear Country. Logistics, logistics, logistics. It was no simple matter to get an attraction of this scope up and going. But of course, Doc was an innovator and worked long hours to make his dream work. The single most prominent reason that Bear Country would be ready and successful for years to come is Doc Casey's love of animals and compassion for enabling them to roam free without the encumbrances of bars and cages, as it should be.

From concept to fulfillment the Bear Country facility was professional in every aspect. Favorable endorsements assured the welfare of the animals. It was but a matter of time before the word was spread about Doc Casey's wild idea that was not so wild afterall. Bear Country USA officially opened in August 26, 1972, a success from the start, albeit a slow start. What remained now was to slowly build up the animal population but not at the risk of endangering any of the species.

At the end of the tourist season of 1972 Bear Country closed down like most of the tourist oriented businesses in the Black Hills. Preparations had been made in advance for the winter upkeep and care of the animals, including the construction of dens so the Black Bears could follow their natural patterns of hibernation and, with good fortune, the birthing of cubs. The outlook was positive. Winter would be spent acquiring more animals, stocking up on supplies and acquiring more and more knowledge pertaining to the habits, quirks and needs of each of them.

Doc heard of some surplus Black Bears at the Brookfield Zoo in Chicago, Illinois. He knew there was a certain protocol that had to be followed if he were to even be considered as the recipient of these bears or any animals, as public, tax supported zoos do not normally transact business with private animal businesses. End of December, 1972, he had a talk with Tal Lockwood, then superintendent of the Department of Game and Parks located in Custer State Park in the Black Hills, south of Rapid City.

Bear Country was thoroughly checked out from every angle, as was Doc. Satisfied that the entire plan and area could only be beneficial to wild animals, Superintendent Lockwood wrote a letter to Dr. Chris Wemmer at Brookfield:

". . . Doctor Casey is at this time working hard at establishing a modern version of a wildlife park. . . . I am confident he will have a high quality operation when it is completed.

"Our zoo here in Custer State Park has been officially closed and some of the animals will be going to Doctor Casey's 'Bear Country'. We feel Doctor Casey is on the right track and would rather see our animals transferred to a high quality undertaking as his.

"I recommend Doctor Casey's Wildlife Park, 'Bear Country' as a proper method of displaying wild animals."

Additional support came from Darrell Brady, Assistant Regional Supervisor:

"Dr. Dennis P. Casey, owner of Bear Country USA here in the Black Hills said you are requiring a reference to insure that Bear Country is a responsible and accepted attraction and the animals will be well cared for.

"I have always been very critical of Zoos in general . . . however, I have visited Bear Country USA and am very impressed by the amount of room the animals have amid the natural surroundings of pine covered hills. Each species of animals is in a different pasture and visitors may drive through on a winding road and view them in their natural habitat, a separate pasture for the buffalo, one for the wolves, another for the bear, etc. I would not even call it a Zoo and am very happy to recommend Bear Country USA as a reputable wildlife attraction."

Dr. Chris Wemmer replied:

"Dear Dr. Casey: On the basis of your correspondence of 5 January 1973 and the two letters of reference, we believe that Bear Country is a reputable and responsible organization."

In late February 1973, Dr. Wemmer arranged to have seven Black Bear cubs safely sent to the Black Hills, their new and comfortable home. They arrived and were a little confused upon their release at their new home but in a matter of time were running, romping and rolling just like any bear would in the wild.

In six short months, Bear Country USA had gone from an "attraction" of local interest to a certified, legitimate entity that had set the standard for drive through wildlife parks. There would be many survey studies conducted in time to come. The Mayo Clinic in Rochester, Minnesota, as an example, when they requested, ". . . the chance to obtain blood and urine samples from female bears hibernating . . . whether they are eating or drinking . . . if urination or defecation is noted and they are certain it is a female bear, we are interested in this and would appreciate a record if possible. . ."

One of the more interesting research projects was a partnership between Bear County and Washington State University in Pullman, Washington. The ultimate goal of this project was to successfully transfer Panda Bear embryos into female Black Bears in order to propagate the Panda out of its endangered species status. This research came about as a result of a graduate student at WSU working on her thesis. The project was terminated without success. A private research group, Bears Incorporated has recently approached Bear Country with a request to continue the project.

Together, Bear Country and Bears Incorporated are the first to try getting the technique down for retrieval and transfer of the embryo. If this can be done in the Black Bear first, then it can possibly be done to the other bears, i.e. the Grizzly Bear embryo transferred into a Black Bear, the Spectacled Bear Embryo into a Black Bear, and so on.

Many bears are endangered, such as the Spectacled Bear and Sun Bear. One problem is that many people do not believe that the Panda is a bear. If this is the case, the Black Bear's system will not accept a Panda embryo. Still, the project is deemed important enough to pursue, and there is always hope in the dream.

These people are not mad scientists. Their credentials lend validity to their quest to save the endangered Panda Bear. Bear Country is the only place in the world where they are able to conduct studies in captive circumstances with a large quantity of female Black Bears. The international ramifications of the very important project is exciting to Bear Country and they are proud indeed to be considered a valuable member of the team.

As recently as the winter of 2000, the habits and health of the Black Bears at Bear Country have been studied. The San Diego Zoo requested and received permission to install hi-tech video filming cameras and infrared lights in six bear dens where pregnant female bears would be sleeping the months away and, hopefully, giving birth to a new generation of cubs. A special building was constructed near the dens to house state of the art sophisticated equipment. This particular project is still active.

Once set up and tested, the cameras rolled and a six to eight month monitoring on TV screens provide a show of the little known activity in the female Black Bear den during hibernation. Primarily, it is a behavior study of the mother/cub interaction in the den. It was all recorded, complete with sound, the crescent position of the female laying on one side virtually unmoving, the birthings of the cubs, softly grunting, eyes still closed while searching for the mother's nipple from which they would noisily suck the life giving, fat and protein milk, growing stronger and more alert each day.

When Bear Country was in the embryonic stages it was practical and necessary to keep some of the younger critters at the Casey home in the valley, owls, wolves, raccoons, bear cubs, foxes and even an occasional mountain lion cub. For the Casey kids it was always fun to have these creatures as playmates. It seemed so natural that to them, petting a dog was no different than petting a mountain lion. Pauline and Doc filmed home movies of the kids sledding, being pulled by a car or motorcycle, and while riding in the sleds, bear cubs would chase them around. Mike Casey said, "At the time it was just the way it was . . . but, wow . . . I wish every kid could grow up in that environment!"

Pauline did not seem to differentiate between the two legged cubs and the four legged cubs. After they are transferred from the dens, about mid-March each year, to the "nursery", each cub gets personal and devoted care. While feeding bear cubs, Pauline would cuddle them in her arms and talk to them just as she did to her own babies at one time. The bears obviously enjoyed the attention and the soothing voice of Pauline as they sucked, gurgled, grunted and cooed with their tiny lips wrapped tightly around the nipple of a bottle full of rich, warm formula. Shannon, the Casey's only daughter, carries on the tradition.

Black bear cubs love to climb. It is a unique experience to be standing in the cub "nursery" several weeks after birth and have one of them wobble over to you and awkwardly climb up your leg until they reach your chest and begin mewing that sounds like a cross between a puppy whining and a purring kitten. A finger or thumb in the mouth quiets them, much like a pacifier soothes a human baby. A leg does nicely as a substitute tree. Even at this early age, bear cubs have claws like needles prompting their human "Nannies" to wear thick trousers.

On one occasion, Doc's namesake, Dennis, was sitting on the living room floor watching TV and some of the young animals wandered freely inside the house. Sean, who was sitting on the couch, also watching TV, noticed the present "Cougar Cub in Residence" hunkering down behind Dennis, assuming the classic attack mode. After some butt and tail twitching, all the while inching closer, it leaped and simultaneously wrapped its front paws around Dennis' face and biting the back of his head.

Sean yelled for Doc, who was on the phone at the time. Doc, in a normal voice, told the person on the other end of the phone, "Hold on just a minute, I gotta take care of something". Still holding the phone, he walked calmly over to where Dennis and the cub were rolling about the floor, whacked the cub on the head and went right back to his phone call. The cub skeedaddled to another part of the house, thwarted, to await its next prey. Dennis was only slightly scratched. He rationalized that the cub probably, seeing the back of Dennis' head and long hair, thought it was a grouse or other prey and natural instinct kicked in.

When Bear Country started showing a few figures in the black, John Vucurevich asked Doc how things were going. Doc told him that he had been offered $250,000 for the operation, lock, stock and barrel. John enthusiastically replied, "Sell it , Casey, sell it!" Of course, Casey was not about to sell.

All of the Casey kids began their working careers, usually about six years old or so, at Bear Country. Doc would start them off standing at the entrance booths with BEAR COUNTRY USA bumper stickers that they would slap, often askew, on the back bumpers of cars when they stopped to pay admission.

The Casey's had no way of formulating the expense of running an operation such as Bear Country. They did manage to keep their heads above water, just below the nostrils, in day to day operations but improvements, acquisitions and expansion were an ongoing necessity. Doc mortgaged his dental office building several times over in the beginning but always repaid the loans.

Doc had some unique, if not strange, ideas about why some animals do what they do. He even did a lot of research. Two examples. Why did Bighorn Sheep get toothaches and why Moose licked metal fences. He had an ingrained curiosity about these things, both as the dentist and as a person who genuinely cared about the welfare of all animals, be they wild or domestic. He never found the answers, as far as anyone knows. His curiosity did not apply to wild animals alone.

Long before the Bear Country idea was hatched, Doc had heard of a farmer in Iowa who had an older herd of milk cows that were not producing or producing very little milk. The farmer's reasoning was that the cow's could not longer chew because they had worn their teeth down to where they could no longer chew up their food and therefore had insufficient intake of grass, grain and the like needed to produce the milk. The farmer had a local dentist put metal caps on the old cow's teeth and soon milk was being squeezed from their teats as good or better than before.

Doc, the dentist, was intrigued. He acquired samples of these so called "cattle caps". He was very excited about this new idea, fully intending to see it through, but for one reason or another, the project never fully developed. So, the innovative dentist went on to some other task, more than once.

One of the things about Doc, often described in the same breath as a genius and/or a crazy man, once an idea was implanted in his brain there was just no way of changing his mind, no matter what. Whether it worked or not, he would always smile just for the fact that he at least tried.

For all that he ever achieved, Doc was never "full of himself" and not one to brag about his accomplishments. Although he knew a lot and was a voracious reader, always learning, he was quick to admit when he did not know something with, "Ya' know, that's another thing, I don't know much about . . ." If you were to see him meandering down the street or strolling about the grounds of Bear Country there was no way of telling that he was a doctor of dentistry and an entrepreneur who conceived and started one of the most popular tourist attractions in the Black Hills. He was perfectly "disguised", attired in his daily wardrobe, plaid shirt, wrinkled pants, scuffed

BEHIND
THE SCENES

boots that never knew polish or brush, and his crumpled, stained, narrow brimmed Stetson perched jauntily on his head.

He preferred to work from behind the scenes, were it helping St. Martin's, the Catholic high school, on a political campaign or doing good deeds, financially and materially for charitable organizations. In essence, Doc was just plain and simple, not interested in taking the credit or getting the glory. He just wanted to get a job done to the best of his ability. Part of his legacy was his word and his integrity.

One of the many "Doc's" kids working for him was Mark Lantis, a young cowboy who went to work in 1985. Mark started out working the Casey cattle on some leased range near Pringle, South Dakota and later at Doc's Mill Iron Ranch south of Wind Cave. The fencing around the Pringle property was in deplorable shape, more fence down than up. The cattle could not distinguish between who owned what and would naturally stray beyond boundary lines, frequently ending up eating the neighbors hay, or be found chomping the grass to the roots in the front yards, leaving piles of manure in their wake.

Mark was constantly apologizing to the neighbors, spending most of his time in the saddle rounding up the strays and herding them back to the Casey pastures. Mark, after several visits to gather up the strays, confronted Doc in a not altogether diplomatic tone of voice. Doc stood, stoic, resting on a leaning fence post, sans fence wire, listening to Mark go on awhile until he paused to take a breath. "Well, what would you do about it, Mark?".

"Seems plain to me", said Mark. "I'd fix up what fence is still fixable and build some new so those damn cows can stay where they belong!"

Smiling the smile, Doc told his hired hand, "I was wonderin' how long it'd take ya' to come up with that idea. Go ahead and build the damn fence!" By letting the other fellow figure it out, Doc gave another lesson.

Not long after this confrontation, Mark was working with Kevin Casey and another hand, rounding up some strays on the Mill Iron Ranch and Mark had ridden way out front, easing a few head down a slight incline

COWHAND

to cross a shallow gully. His horse was stopped but the angle caused it to lose its front feet. It tumbled head down, tossing its rump up and over making it impossible for Mark to clear the saddle and the full crushing weight of the horse landed on him before rolling off.

Mark was free of the saddle now but he knew he was in trouble when he tried to move only to be slammed back to the earth by excruciating pains streaking through his back and pelvis. He managed to coax the horse, with a couple of painful rock tosses, back to the top of the slope where a good while later, Kevin spotted it and came to Mark's assistance.

Once an ambulance could make its way to the scene, Mark was stabilized and rushed to the hospital where he was found to have severe internal bleeding and a break in his pelvis that turned it to mush. Doc hurried to the hospital as soon as he heard about the accident. After talking with Mark's mother, Julie Lantis, he went in to see Mark. "How you feelin', boy?" Mark assured him he was not feeling real good.

"Damn it, I've told you boys time and again not ride so damn fast!" Mark said the horse was practically standing still at the time. Doc came back, "You were tossed, weren't you? Then you musta been goin' too damn fast!" At that Doc started crying, sad for the hurt but glad Mark, one of the many in his extended family, was alive.

The story of Doc Casey cannot be complete without describing some of his personal habits, quirks and obsessions. First, although not foremost was his "office". In the words of Gordon Magusson:

". . . I could drop in on Dennis in his (gasp, choke) 'office' (har-dee-har-har) and sit with him, listening to his daily philosophical positions and his intensely vocalized political opinions of local, regional, national and international politics. One of the things that he would mention at almost every one of our visits was how proud he was of his children, and how little he understood his wife (with a twinkle in his eye and the trademark Casey grin!)

"Dennis told me over and over again about Pauline's ability to accomplish whatever needed to be done. He admired her spunk.

"An important part of these visits would be the exchange of the latest joke that each of us had heard, with the obligatory slap on the knee, bellowing guffaw, and shake of the head by me after Dennis completed his anecdote."

The "office" was a corner of the employee snack area where they would punch the time clock and get their working orders from Doc and later from the Casey boys. Doc sat behind a gray surplus military desk that was covered with mounds of bills, political journals, recipes for feeding animals, vials of tranquilizers (presumably for the animals), maps, knick knacks, half eaten doughnuts, a coffee cup with what appeared to be a dark thick mud at the bottom and an ashtray overflowing

OBSESSIONS

with butts. The resident mouse would be seen sometimes as it scurried across the desk under the papers and boxes sniffing out doughnut crumbs or God knows what else might had been buried beneath it all or how long it had been there.

Here, the coffee was always on. There could never be a complete conversation with Doc without either the phone ringing or when one of his employees would come in to ask him a question about this or that. Doc would listen, sort out the problems and with a few words would move the person in the right direction. It would be also from here that Doc would field customer complaints. He was a natural at handling people.

If someone would loudly complain about a bear scratching their car or trying to lick the chrome from their bumpers, Doc would patiently listen until folks would get it out of their systems. "Yeah", he would say with a grin, "those critters do like the taste of car!" After his calming humor, Doc would proceed to visit with the complainer, now a friend, and then make any damages good.

The office/desk area is now Kevin's space and is being faithfully maintained by him with occasional cluttering by the other Casey boys as well as the hired help. Doc would have been proud - there is more debris than before. It is but a matter of time before historical preservation funds can be applied for assuring a place in history for the desk, if the area is not first condemned by the Pennington County Sanitation Department.

Then, there were Doc's pickups. Again, the colorful words of Gordon Magusson:

". . . anyone can have a bright, shiny, new and clean pickup. It takes sheer grit and iron-bound determination to drive a truck that is never washed except by God's good cleanser of the world, rain, and good ol' South Dakota hail to occasionally knock off large clumps of gumbo mud welded to the fenders, running boards and bumpers.

"It was possible to write one's name in the dash board dirt after parting the litter on the dash board, litter which, when Dennis would take a corner too fast, would fall to the floor to mix with the assorted junk already there.

"The windows were commonly down . If rolled up, the outside world became fuzzy. The windshield was, in itself, a triumph, representing at long last a correct artistic interpretation of the Biblical phrase, 'Now we see through the glass darkly'.

"I was never certain of what that strange coating was on all of the windows or if it was on the outside or inside. If, however, the windows would be rolled up, there was a proven probability that various objects such as trees, posts, fire trucks and odd buildings would approach his pickup and place a collection of dents therein and thereupon!

"Now, there was a pickup!

"The frosting on the cake was, however, not a part of the pickup but was Dennis himself, leaning out of his side window with his talcum-powder color "Open Road" Stetson pulled down low over the brow and canted slightly to one side as he would pause, having recognized me or another of his many friends and would say, 'Hi! Whatcha' up to?', with that, elflike Irish grin!"

Pauline was sitting in her office one day in 1981 when she answered a phone call from Atlanta, Georgia. The caller said that a Mr. Turner wished to speak to her about the possibility of buying two Black Bear cubs for a private wildlife reserve on an island off the coast of the Carolinas.

After chatting for a bit, Pauline explained what had to be done before any animals could be shipped, the price, etc., Mr. Turner agreed to the terms and asked how soon the cubs could be shipped. Pauline said, "Just as soon as we receive your check."

Mr. Turner politely said, "Do you know who this is? My word is good."

"Yes, you told me, you're Mr. Ted Turner. And I am certain that your word is good. But I still need a check before shipping our cubs to you." She was all business.

After some more chit-chat, Mr. Turner said that he would have his secretary send a check that day. She did and the bears were later shipped. Later, on the day of the phone call, Pauline was telling Doc about the conversation.

WHO?

He asked her who it was again that called. She told him again. Doc sputtered and stammered, "My God, Pauline, he's a rich man. His credit's good! Haven't you ever heard of the Atlanta Braves or CNN?"

"Well, I still need a check first. And besides, we don't have cable."

Doc walked away, scratching his head while shaking it at the same time, chuckling to himself about how Pauline refused to give credit to Mr. Ted Turner! About ten years later, Ted Turner visited Bear Country. He was visiting with Brendan Casey out in the field looking over the operation. Later, Doc introduced Pauline to Turner. She said, "Now, I know who you are!"

Turner came back with, "I know, I know, I have to send my check first!" They all got a laugh out of this.

There have been many human celebrities visiting Bear County over the years. Bear Country has had its own celebrities, of the animal variety. One of the bears, "Casey", was a prime actor in the 1997 Disney movie, "The Jungle Book". "Casey" is proud of this achievement but prefers to remain anonymous so as not to make the other bears jealous. He is now retired and resides in California.

The most famous bear is "Coconino". She was the center of the biggest bear cub custody battle in history. She was taken from the wild near Big Bear, California by hikers and hand raised by a veterinarian and his wife. When the California Department of Fish and Game found this out, they wanted the cub back. What ensued was a national media frenzy. The citizens of Big Bear formed a campaign to find "Coco" a suitable new home.

She was featured on the TV show, "Hard Copy" three times in 1990. Finally, by ruling of the court, "Coco" was given to Bear Country USA, where she arrived under the media's watchful eye. Since then, she has been visited by many of the residents from the community

CELEBRITIES

of Big Bear. They all seem to agree that "Coco" is now in the best possible place and many have written letters thanking Bear Country for taking "Coco" in. She still lives free at Bear Country where she can easily be spotted, a cinnamon colored bear with a split right ear.

"All animals, big and small, deserve our respect and our compassion." That is the message that Bear Country USA wants to convey and encourage you, me and everyone "to do whatever you can to ensure that all species of animals will be around for our children and children's children to enjoy. Never forget . . . extinct is forever!"

Doc's dental practice and the grueling responsibilities and long hours at Bear Country soon took a toll on Doc. Recreational drinking became a daily need. And it did not help that Doc so thoroughly enjoyed the company of his many friends and drinking buddies he would meet nightly at one of several "watering holes" where they would quaff several rounds before the night ended. Also, he was smoking two to three packs a day, searing and etching, puff by puff, the irreversible blueprint for emphysema.

There are as many Doc stories about his capacity for drink, as there are about his wonderful sense of humor, his grin and his total lack of pretentiousness, both often told in conjunction with the other. "He was a drinker", one person put it, "but never a drunk!" His own family said of Doc that he was not an obnoxious, abusive or "falling down" drunk but they could not help but be aware of the consistent drinking and irratic behavior ever on the increase. It was obviously and painfully apparent to them, to others and to Doc himself that Doc needed help. Doc was an alcoholic.

Kevin Casey said in his father's eulogy:

". . . They married and stayed by each other's side and stayed in love through it all. It wasn't easy. With two personalities like these there was bound to be some fireworks and some nights where dad called the couch his bed. It may not have looked like a great relationship from the outside, but it was. Even though a pain in the rear sometimes, she will tell you, he was her best friend." And he was.

Pauline, with the advice and help of some of their friends and acquaintances who were also alcoholics, convinced Doc to seek treatment

CONFRONTATION

at the local chapter of the Alcoholics Anonymous. He did but only with moderate success. On December 21, 1977, Doc asked two AA buddies to fly with him to Minneapolis and help him check in to St. Mary's Hospital for rehabilitation. Within hours, they had Doc on a private plane enroute to Minneapolis. He was there for a month. It was not a Merry Christmas. Doc's immediate family as well as his siblings were required to be present for a week of confrontational counseling during the treatment.

With the exception of the two very young Casey children, Mike and John, and Doc's sister, Virginia, they all were there. The atmosphere was charged from the beginning. Doc did not help matters any. He had become very skillful at denying he had a problem with alcohol, clouding the issues with words and head games. Each time he was confronted, he would riposte with a nervous laugh, avoiding eye contact with his family and the therapist.

The Casey's, crammed into a small stuffy room, seemed eager to escape the reality of Doc's problems. As the session wore on, some of them mentally confronted their own personal problems of one sort or another. The therapy was designed to open emotional wounds. In doing so, nothing was sacred.

Toward the end of the sessions, the humor of Jack Casey, Doc's brother, helped to defuse a potentially damaging rift among the clan members when one of them attacked another, goading her into "opening up" with her own problems. Jack told the story this way:

"Well, you know, Dennis had a little trouble with alcohol - we all got troubles with something now, don't we? We all went over to his alcohol treatment in Minneapolis, sisters and brothers. One brother, Jerry, came from Watertown with a beat up old car that didn't amount to much. Another brother, Ed, came from Minneapolis. His car had been smashed in the side by a pickup. The heater didn't work as a result. So, when we'd all get in his car in the cold winter early mornings to go to the treatment thing, Jerry would have trouble seeing what with all of our breaths frostin' up the windows and his defroster not working. He also had trouble with the transmission so's the car would hardly go.

"My sister, Dee, from Denver was there. She had to get back to Denver that particular day. The counselor at the rehab place said, 'Delores, do you have to catch a plane at eleven o'clock?' Dee replied back, 'Yes, I do.' 'Have you got wheels to get to the airport?'

"Everyone busted out laughing." 'Wheels, we got! Transmissions 'n' heaters we're short of . . .!'"

In addition to his individual and group alcohol counseling, Doc was involved on several occasions in a grief group to assist him in dealing with the death his firstborn son, David. At one point, the group and the group psychiatrist became very concerned with Doc's intensity about David's death. Upon completion of the group sessions, remarks indicated that the program seemed very effective for Doc, and "that he appeared to be able to accept David's death, without blaming his wife, the physician or God any longer".

Here, as in AA meetings back in Rapid, Doc had just the measure of "grandiosity" that prevented him from making decisions to fully participate and he would frequently create a ruckus with word manipulations and inappropriate giggles. One exceptionally concerned and faithful friend kept trying to get Doc to attend the Rapid City AA meetings and probably tried to "12-Step" him a lot but the demon of drink was always one step ahead.

1984 would see Doc being admitted for a second alcohol treatment program, this time at the Heartview Clinic in North Dakota. This time only Pauline and the seven Casey children would take part in the family treatment session. Collectively and individually, each of them were engulfed in a shroud of stress. Here was their father, for a second time, being treated for alcoholism and they had to confront it head on. Through words, not always kind, and many a tear shed, they made it through what was a week of hell for everyone. It was painful. Truth often is. Whether they knew it or not, Doc was suffering all of their pain along with his.

Doc always thought things out. His family and some friends would be impatient with him when they believed that certain things should be done "now". Doc would think ahead, plain and simple. To others, Doc appeared to be going up a wrong road to a dead end, but then, they could never see what he saw. Often, if one of his kid's plans differed from his, Doc would tell them, without mincing words, "It'll never work." And if it did work, he would seldom acknowledge it. Folks would ask his opinion on a variety of issues, to which he would reply, "After two drunk tanks and three marriage counselors, I still don't have the answers." But when it came to the operation of Bear Country, he seemed to have all the answers which sometimes proved frustrating for all concerned.

Both Pauline and Doc wanted children, a family. They were blessed with seven, six boys and one girl. Each would learn the need and importance of honesty and integrity, raised knowing full well that their parents would not stand for any deviation from the truth. All of the children would be genetically endowed with "Irishism".

Pauline's kin are still living in Ballygar, Ireland, near Galway. One branch, the Kennys, still runs the local pub, now managed by Tommy Kenny. Pauline and the Kennys stay in touch and in the near future, Pauline and the Casey kids are going to visit their Irish cousins. Sadly, Doc, who once said a trip to Ireland would be his ideal vacation, will not be with them.

The firstborn, after David's death, was Kevin in 1961. He is a graduate of Carroll College in Helena, Montana where he earned his degree in Biology. As the oldest, he became, naturally, the heir apparent to the ranching end of the Casey holdings, as well as Bear Country. The other Casey offspring agree that Kevin was most like Doc in many ways, in his gestures and generosity. From the time he could walk, Kevin wanted to be a cowboy. When he was two years old, he constantly wore a cowboy hat and cowboy boots. His favorite toy was a rocking horse that he would ride with reckless abandon while urging it with "giddyups" to a realistic gallop as only the imagination of youth can do.

Today, Kevin is responsible for all animal health related issues, all ranching activities (cattle, buffalo, elk), research activities with outside organizations,

PROGENY

acquisition of animals and dealing with government agencies involving inspections and regulations for animals. Unofficially, he is competing with Doc for the "really bad" pickup award.

Kevin manages the Casey's Mill Iron ranch, located just south of and adjoining Wind Cave National Park. There are some 17,000 deeded and 25,000 leased acres to the Mill Iron. The entire area is surrounded with high sturdy fencing to keep their large herd of Bison from straying. As docile as these shaggy beasts appear, they possess great strength and speed, and are capable of inflicting great harm.

In 1997, the family had a fair size herd of Elk, purchased from out of state and raised over the years with plans to start the wild game processing program. The Elk herd had been thoroughly tested utilizing required, rigid guidelines. After they were turned out to pasture, the Elk started acting far from normal. A veterinarian was called in, and the diagnosis was not good. They had obviously contacted Chronic Wasting Disease, CWD, a disease peculiar to Elk and deer.

Doc was always testing the hell out of every animal he purchased. He did not want any disease in any of his animals. There is not, however, a known test for CWD, except for a dead animal. It can take as long as seven years for the disease to show up once it is contacted. Every Elk had to be destroyed, a huge setback for the Casey Elk project. Kevin, only recently, acquired more elk and is hoping that they remain healthy and productive.

Dennis, Doc's namesake, as the other Casey kids, did his time at Bear Country. When he was a teenager, girls would call Bear Country and ask for Dennis. If Doc would answer the phone, he would always ask, "Which one, the rich one or the good lookin' one?"
"The good looking one!"
    "Speaking!"
    After getting his BS in Psychology and Business Administration from Carroll College in 1986, Dennis fulfilled an old itch to travel. Before settling down, he wandered about in thirteen countries and admits that through the sharing of many cultures, he probably learned more about living and giving than he had learned before or since. He later chose not to work at Bear Country mainly because of his interest in any business involving vehicles.

Dennis had an idea to start a used automobile business combined with the rentals of used cars and passenger vans. Doc may have wanted all of his kids to be a permanent part of Bear Country, but he appreciated their independent streaks. In 1979, Doc bought a corner lot from an old mechanic, Lloyd, who used to work at Bear Country and would also work on the Casey's cars and trucks. Situated on the lot was a service station converted to a two-stall garage with an adjoining office suitably described as "grungy". A fire had gutted the building, and it sat empty for eight years or so after Doc bought it.

Lloyd was not what one would term as a real good mechanic

but good enough to keep engines running. He was sort of slow and a bit overweight, his large frame usually draped in coveralls coated with grease and oil. Lloyd was a good soul, one of the many people Doc had befriended. He, in turn, befriended the Casey boys, although he knew full well that some of them would pilfer candy from the automatic dispenser in his shop. It is widely believed that Lloyd was kept working solely to keep Doc's "crap" collection of junk cars and tractors in semi-operating condition. Doc's generosity spilled over into the lives of many such people.

Dennis started cleaning up the place in late 1988, putting in long hours. After a thorough cleansing, he spent his nights working on the ceiling and walls, entirely redoing the interior until it was ready to open in the spring of 1989. Doc would come by and check in on Dennis and pound a few nails from time to time until was too weak from his emphysema to get out of the truck. On each of his visits Dennis would be treated to "Docisms".

"How's it goin'?" meaning if there had been any sales. Or, usually in the spring, "How's the summer smellin'?" meaning how many reservations were there for rental cars in the prime summer season. Dennis always had an internal drive to show his dad financial statements and tax returns for the previous year, lean or rich. Doc would look the statements and returns over, carefully, taking his time. On the bad ones, he would simply say, "Be careful". On the good years, he would say, "You're goin' in the right direction". Translation, "Trim the fat" or "Increase the revenue."

Brendan Casey's education background varies somewhat from the other siblings. He attended Marquette University in Milwaukee, Wisconsin, starting out in pre-dental but switched over to Carroll College to degree in Biology and Chemistry. Marketing, construction, park personnel, vehicle and equipment purchasing and maintenance and liability and commercial insurance matters are part of his responsibilities. In addition, Brendan keeps current on the legal end of land issues, handles cash and deposits from ticket booth and is first in line to field visitor complaints or damages, bestowing upon him the title of "Assistant Schmoozer", second only to the Chief "Schmoozer", Pauline, affectionately known as "Ma Bear".

Sean shares the title of "Imagineer" with Brendan. His sense of humor, on the dry and oft times wry side balances his serious work side. Figures are his forte as he works with park personnel, marketing, accounting, utilities systems, financial planning, keeping corporate records and managing investment income and bank accounts. He graduated from South Dakota School of Mines in 1988 with a BS in Computer Sciences, and utilizes his skills to keep this end of the business up and running.

Sean was often away from the desk in last months of 2000 and for several months of 2001 and 2002 to oversee the energetic undertaking of the new "Babyland" and visitor amphitheater construction, a tribute to the desire and pledge of the Casey's to continuously update and improve the Bear Country USA facilities and attractions. Sean said that Doc is probably "up there" freaking out over the magnitude of these new additions.

Before getting his degree, Sean had aced out some other Tech students for a position as a Computer Systems Analyst with the Mobil Oil Corporation and would be working in Denver. He was justifiably excited. It was a splendid opportunity for a young person. He told his dad about the job that he had just won. Doc flared, "What the hell, this is too damn much! You have to finish your education!" Sean went on to explain that he was still required to finish college, then Doc thought it was a great idea. Was it the fact that Sean would not finish college that bothered Doc or the idea of a 20 year old moving to Denver by himself?

Doc had retired from his dental practice in 1991. Bear Country, by now, had become a major business. Doc was pretty good about giving up responsibilities and letting his kids make their own decisions but never let them forget that he had the supreme veto power. He always said that all he cared about was "weeds and trees", and he would leave the rest to the others. Not entirely true. Doc's health and physical condition had worsened, and was more than likely responsible for his mixed messages of wanting/not wanting to give up responsibility. This was beginning to irritate not only his family up at Bear Country but a few of the other workers as well.

Kevin, Brendan and Sean were running the park at the time, but Doc could not let go of his life's work. One day the tenseness came to a head. Brendan became red-faced angry with Doc and told him that he was quitting. For whatever reason, Doc was especially hard on Brendan, sometimes deserved, sometimes not. Brendan usually ignored Doc's remarks but his own Irish temper flared. He stormed out the door to the parking lot where Sean caught up with him. "Please, 'Brendie', don't do this? Stay strong, man. I can't last here without you and I need you to keep fighting!" Brendan agreed to think the quitting idea through. At the same time, Doc was making some of the best employees feel stupid and inadequate. Some of them were threatening to also quit. It was one of those times when everything seemed to be absolutely crazy and in dire need of damage control.

Sean coaxed Doc into his car and they drove up to the Gaslight Restaurant in Rockerville. Whereas the father used to confront the son, the opposite was now painfully occurring. Sean explained to Doc that several important people, essential to the continued operation of Bear Country, were about to quit and point blank asked him if he wanted them to run the place or not.

It was a heart wrenching confrontation. All of the Casey kids have a sensitive part of their soul as well as a portion lent to anger. In the end, their ability to reason and rationalize enabled them to compromise and arrive at equitable solutions to just about any problem. Here sat two men talking it out, tears streaking their cheeks for different reasons but with one meaning. One was sick and surely feeling "left out" in decision making for the business he had started for his kids. The other was suddenly thrown into the grownup world of supervision and responsibility necessitated by the survival of that business.

Not a pretty picture. By talking it out with the reinforcement of their love for one another and the release of built up anguish and anger through the cleansing power of tears. The situation was defused for the time being and Doc basically agreed to let the family run Bear Country and he would retire. Brendan did cool down and returned to work.

And then, there is Shannon, the only daughter of Pauline and Doc. Doc would always refer to her as, "The best looking daughter I have". For Shannon, growing up in a clan of six boys and a chauvinist father was a lesson in survival. While she was growing up, some of the Casey lads would pick on her, sometimes roughing her up. She bided her time, waiting until she got older and tougher, then she started hitting back. More than one Casey boy regretted their previous treatments of their sister.

The all male environment put an edge on her that probably would not have been there otherwise. That edge, in part, makes her who she is. Doc was always there for her, her friend whenever she needed him, as he was also with his boys. In reality, a self professed "male Chauvinist pig", Doc understood women more than he gave himself credit for, but, of course, he never credited himself for anything. To Shannon, Doc was more of a presence, an all encompassing man.

Shannon commented that, "Dad's alcoholism was difficult. When dad was on his death bed, I actually thanked him for being an alcoholic. It is part of what made me who I am today, and I like the person I have become. The two treatment sessions we went to helped shape me. They made me a strong, confident person and helped me understand the dynamics of human relationships and personalities.

"Had he not received help and treatment, I am sure his disease would had done much more damage to our family. Whenever we were in treatment, I was always thankful that he was more of an 'intellectual alcoholic' than one who would beat and abuse us. I honestly believe that had Dad not been an alcoholic, we would not have Bear Country . . . I don't think that he would have had the guts to do it.

"He was surely a tough person to live with at times and almost impossible to get praise from (he always praised us to others but rarely to us). But, he was a very fair father and he was always there for all of us."

Shannon graduated from St. Martin's Academy in Rapid City, as did her siblings. After two years at Carroll College she did a fall semester at Creighton before spending her spring 1989 semester with the "Semester at Sea" program through the University of Pittsburgh. In her words, it was "AWESOME! It opened my mind to the world and I received 12 credits to boot!" She, as her brother Dennis, inherited Doc's love of travel, believing that it was good for a person's mind and soul. She returned to Carroll for her final year, 1989 finishing with a BA in Business Administration. She was 3 credits shy of her BA in International Relations but had a "falling out" with one of her instructors, so she told him, "What he could do with and where he could put his degree!"

No doubt about it, she's Irish.

Today, Shannon is the retail manager of the gift shop at Bear Country. She keeps busy with purchasing and inventory, as well as overseeing gift shop operations and assists with trade shows and special events. But her real love is organizing the baby animal feeding, participating herself, talking to the little ones just as her mom did. She raises the little ones until they are old enough to eat "big" food out of a dish, training young women on how to feed and take care of the bear and wolf cubs. Much of the time, Shannon takes the baby foxes, coyotes, lynx, cougars and even beaver home to raise. As with her brothers, she has gained a lot of discipline, responsibility, nurturing and love of nature through all of this.

Mark Ballard planned to propose to Shannon while on vacation in the Grand Caymans where they were going to vacation with some friends. Shortly before they departed, Mark "wanted to do the right thing" and ask her parents, specifically Doc's permission. Mark called, talking first with Pauline who was very excited. That was encouraging.

When Doc came on line, Mark asked if he could "have Shannon's hand in marriage." There was a long, long pause. Sweat time. Doc then replied, "I don't know why you are asking me. As far as I see it, that's your problem!" Mark was treated to Doc Casey's sense of humor, sardonic, at times warped, but always with good intentions. Mark and Shannon married and now have a son, "Casey".

Second youngest, Mike, also did his stint at Bear Country. He probably enjoyed the "bumper sticker" days best of all his duties. When he was 18 or so, Doc told him to go up into the "Bear Tower" where the compound could be observed to assure that there were not problems with the animals or the tourists. "That is a chicken boy job," Mike told an irritated Doc who had raised his kids to do every job, with little regard to the importance of it. As soon as he had made the remark, Mike regretted doing so and climbed up to the observation tower anyway. Meanwhile, although he was not in very good health at the time, just to make a point, Doc decided to climb the long way up to the tower to teach his son a lesson. Mike, of course, was already there, mulling over a lesson about attitude.

Mike received his BS Degree in Computer Sciences from the

South Dakota School of Mines in 1996. He now works at the Rapid City Regional Hospital as a Senior Programmer Analyst. It is a job that he excels in and enjoys.

Mike is asthmatic. When he was younger, it would be quite severe at times. Doc also had asthma pretty bad. There was a clinic in Denver specializing in the treatment of asthma and the family thought it would be a good place for both Doc and Mike to check out. Doc, on his own, although realizing that his asthma was debilitating at times, but too stubborn to admit it, would probably not have gone. He agreed to go, taking Mike, "Because Mike would feel better having me there."

Mike believes his five siblings still at Bear Country are doing a great job in keeping things looking and running good. He has an insight into his family life and background that comes from being a part that is now standing back and observing. Profoundly, he feels, "Everyone has personality quirks whether they are in your family, friends or people you meet on the street. I think it is easier to dismiss the quirks of friends, acquaintances and strangers than those of family. Perhaps, we set higher standards and expect more from family than we really need to."

The youngest Casey is John. He and Mike, close in age, had a lot of fun growing up together. And, in unity there is strength considering the older siblings might have exercised their places in the "pecking order", as they sometimes did. John can walk into a room without being noticed. He is quiet, sensitive and a helpful, honest person. Since he was fourteen, he wanted to work at and be a part of Bear Country. His first supervisory job was reorganizing and managing the snack bar, at the time a "hole in the wall". Understand, here was John, shy, quiet and carrying the accomplishments and mistakes of five brothers, a sister, mom and Doc upon his shoulders. He must have felt that they were all watching, judging him, waiting for him to screw up. And they probably were.

John is a graduate of South Dakota State University at Brookings and has his BS in Business. He is presently in charge of all concessions, concession personnel, co-webmaster and ground crew foreman which entails management and preservation of trees. Like Doc, he hates weeds! At first, John would not dig right in but asked his older brothers what should be done to make various ideas work. His training was received on the job. He would often run a new idea by his siblings who would say,

"Well, try it, John and see if it works!" He would try and it more than likely would work. Innovation comes of necessity, and John, with a new sense of confidence is becoming very innovative. He is still quiet but his works speak for him.

Overall, each of the Caseys pretty much know what the other does at Bear Country. It is part of the organization planning and effort to assure the smoothest possible operation of the family business. They do not always agree with each other. Ideas are hashed out at weekly meetings where the family sits at a table to discuss new projects, budgeting, improvements on existing facilities, acquisitions, maintenance, sales and the animal's welfare. The end results are usually reached through these meetings.

All of them, at one time, wanted to walk away from Bear Country, feeling that they were being unfairly treated with menial tasks and low pay, but mostly because Doc would never openly compliment them or else he would "put them down" by what they interpreted as the demeaning of some of their ideas. As each of them reached that magic plateau in life where maturity and reasoning kicks in, they began to realize why Doc did what he did primarily cause he was Doc. They quit looking for reasons after awhile and shortly came acceptance. What they did know was that their father loved each of them in his own way and perhaps that was enough.

Whenever someone would ask them if they were Doc Casey's kid, they would reply "yes". That person would then immediately break into a story about how Doc had touched and left his magic mark on their lives. It might have been someone that he had met only once but it impressed them in a way that they remembered him as they related to a "Doc" story with a shine in their eyes and a nostalgic smile on their face. And the stories were basically the same. He showed them how to live life with integrity, honesty, charity and courage. Whoever you were, when you were with Doc Casey, you were made to feel special.

Doc had a burning desire to "teach everyone else's kids", how to work hard and be honest but have fun at the same time. The seed of what he did and how he did it, regardless of how it appeared to be at the time, has blossomed in the individual commitment of the clan to carry on and fulfill his desire and taking it a full step further in assuring that Bear

Country will give more back to the community at large.

Regressing, it is a wonder that any of the Casey's remained with Bear Country. Doc kept them on the go, even on their days off. Doc's other pet peeve, besides the weeds, was cigarette butts anywhere on the grounds, especially in the parking lots. He would spy one of the kids or other employees, walking up to them with his, "Whatcha got goin'?" line and at once set them about picking up butts. Yanking weeds became a task all wished to avoid. When they would see Doc approaching, most of the workers would scramble for cover but he would find them. "Whatcha got goin'?".

Doc sensed their frustration and no doubt sympathized, but weeds were weeds and the everlasting enemy of Doc Casey. It would take some enticing to get those boys and girls out there in the war against weeds. One day, before everyone reported to work, Doc went out in a particularly heavy weeded field and tied a twenty dollar bill to one of the taller weeds. Before anyone could sneak off after the morning briefing, Doc announced that "weed killers" would be rewarded with the twenty dollar bill if they found it. Doc 20, Weeds 0!

Life with Doc was a continuing education course in which the Casey clan would never stop learning. He figured that each experience could be positive, and it never really mattered to him what the kids did just as long as they were okay afterwards and had learned something.

One of the questions in the book, A Father's Legacy, was, "What events in life have strengthened your belief in prayer?" To which, Doc replied, "This thing I am going through right now. (his illness). Watching you kids work together on the estate. I believe that you can be fair and honest with each other. Hope each of you can come out with things you want. It won't be exactly even but if you hang together over the years, it will be damn good for all of you. And that is what I pray for . . ."

Doc was beginning to park his pickup closer to his snack bar office at Bear Country. When he would get out of the truck, before going inside, Doc would often lean on the cab, look about, take several unfulfilling breaths and walk slowly inside. He never walked very far anymore. These were the first symptoms of just how severe his physical problems had become, only to be recognized later in the always too late vision of hindsight.

He made frequent visits to the doctors. They probed and poked and had him suck and blow on gadgets that measured the capacity and ability of his lungs to capture precious oxygen and dispose of carbon dioxide. With each visit, the prognosis, while at first not mentioned by the medical people, became more and more evident to Doc himself. More than once, he wanted to quit going in, doing the same tests, answering the same questions. Doc already knew the answers.

Sometime around 1995, Doc began to carry a small green metal bottle full of oxygen that, for the time being at least, assisted with his breathing as it flowed through a clear plastic tube into two very irritating prongs in his nostrils. The cumbersome cylinder became an extension of Doc's being, irritating, probably an embarrassment for such a proud man, but even Doc knew, essential to his mobility.

Doc's pickup became his legs. Sometimes, he would drive up to Bear Country or visit Dennis at his car lot. To anyone he saw, he would stop, lean out of the window and sparingly speak in cadence with the rasping rhythm of the flow of oxygen, "How's it goin'?" Much of his

GOIN' HOME

pickup time, he spent alone driving around his Mill Iron ranch, the "Crown Jewel" of his acreage. Here, he was always most comfortable with himself. Here he could, at least for awhile, ponder his future, his family's future and the future of Bear Country. Here, Doc could, no doubt, reflect on his life, his accomplishments, and perhaps on those things that he never completed. Quite possibly, more than once, he would look his mortality in the eye and consign himself to the inevitable. He accepted it but it was not on his terms so he was not happy about it.

On his last hospital stay, a defiant and demanding Doc insisted that the pesky prongs be removed from his nostrils. Not only were they irritating and inconvenient, he did not seem to be breathing as well as he could and wanted to. His doctor, performed a tracheotomy procedure, inserting a breathing tube into the tracheal airway permitting a direct flow of oxygen to his lungs. Doc's mood and breathing improved, for the time being.

In November 1998, Doc was brought home to the valley where Pauline and the kids watched over him. Before Doc went home, Dr. Rawson gathered the Casey's together in the hospital meeting room. Here, he told them that Doc's illness was terminal and that he probably only had a couple of months. Immediate arrangements were made for Hospice care at home. Hospice care, even with the visits of nurses and care attendants, was not easy and did not get any better. Doc realized this. He had been home four months when, without the knowledge of his family, he made the decision to move into assisted living. He made all of the arrangements himself with the help of his hospice nurse, Julie Lantis. Two days before Saint Patrick's Day, 1999, Doc became a resident at the Victorian Assisted Living facility in Rapid City. He remained there fourteen months. Doc had thus far outlived the doctor's prognosis of life expectancy.

Doc had, for lack of a more descriptive word, "bullshitted" his doctors into believing that he had told Pauline and the kids. Typical Doc. Shannon thought, tearfully, back to one day in 1997 when her father, who knew then that he was dying, insisted that she go with her husband, Mark who was assigned to Tokyo, Japan, where she could see, experience and learn something new.

Each of the seven Casey kids took shifts at the Victorian, one each day of the week, helping to care for their Patriarch. The work of cleaning and sterilizing the "trac" tubing, changing Doc's bed clothing, assisting with his feedings and other necessary tasks were tiring and demanding duties that were willingly, without complaint, and lovingly done day in and day out. When the family would not be able to attend to Doc, the caring and dedicated staff of the Victorian tended to Doc's needs. Doc, sick as he was, still had a way about him that endeared him to all of the staff.

Patti Urban, who attended Doc at the Victorian, wrote a letter to the Caseys: "Who could have thought that knowing one man and his family for only one year could impact a life so greatly as you have mine. . . I have so much gratitude in my heart that I was given the opportunity to care for him! It is so-o easy to care for someone who accepts you for who you are and what you have to give . . . Doc was such a fighter, the whole way . . . Doc would insist, in his healthier moments, that I take home some buffalo sausage. I'd say, 'Doc, you gave me one a couple of weeks ago!' He'd say, 'No, you take it! You've got kids!'. . . Doc showed me such character of strength during a time of weakness in a man . . .

"I was thinking today about Jesus on the cross when He said, 'It is finished'. I will always cherish the moments Doc shared with me when he knew he was finished . . . all things were accomplished in his life. He had settled things with God and was ready to go home. I was so humbled, honored and broken inside when he asked me to pray to Jesus to take him home.

"Thank you for your generosity which speaks of how great your life is. Your are an amazing family, full of love, always giving and thinking of others."

About the middle of May 2000, Julie Lantis, Doc's hospice nurse, received a call from the Victorian. Doc was not doing well. While Julie was sitting at Doc's side, she asked him if there were anything that she could do for him. Doc weakly replied, "Please tell everyone that I love them."

On May 24, 2000, Dennis Patrick Casey died. He was by himself when he passed but he was not alone. When the angels escorted him to heaven, the first person to greet him, grinning a familiar Irish grin, was David, whose first words surely were, "It's okay father . . . it has always been okay." And Doc, for the first time in many years, took a full, satisfying breath of sweet air.

There were over 700 mourners crowded into the Cathedral of Our Lady of Perpetual Help to honor and bid farewell to Dennis Patrick Casey, and to comfort, as best they could, his family. It was later learned that many more came for the Mass of Christian Burial but left because there was no place to park and no room inside the cathedral, and the weather conditions discouraged some from attending.

It was still foggy for so late in the morning. The people came slowly in, greeting one another with a nod, a handshake, an awkward smile through closed lips, fearing that if they smile, exposing their teeth, it might dishonor the deceased. Those would be the ones who did not know Doc Casey well. He would have appreciated the smiles. But, it is difficult to smile when facing the reality of mortality that materializes with the death of someone close to you.

When the Mass was nearly finished, and tears had streaked the cheeks of even the most stoic of mourners, the sky darkened. A light drizzle suddenly became a staccato of rain drops pounding nosily on the roof of the cathedral. Father Zandri, a good friend of the Casey Clan, paused and looked heavenward. A large grin, teeth exposed, lit up the house. "You know what that is, folks?! That is the tears of God. . . God just does not know what to do with the likes of Dennis Patrick Casey!"

The tension was broken. Those in attendance now had permission to smile, laugh and recall the happy times with and stories about Doc. Kevin, the oldest Casey kid now felt better about his eulogy that spoke, in part, "Webster's defines a friend as a person attached to another by respect or affection. If you think that, it will probably remind you of the Doc that you knew.

"The road along the way was at times bumpy. The father and friend became as a brother who, in all three roles was always there for us, always."

The final thanks of the eulogy and to Doc ended in a story about Kevin and some friends in high school out joy riding in his Grandma Foley's Buick Riviera and had stopped at a train crossing. The train passed and Kevin tried to see just how much tire smoke he could generate, not knowing at the time Doc was in his pickup on the other side of the tracks with Dennis and Brendan.

Kevin "spun out", in the middle of an impressive burnout when he looked over to see his Dad in the pickup. Doc was looking straight ahead but Kevin, his eyes wide with fear, saw Dennis and Brendan had spotted him. Doc, still looking forward, not knowing it was Kevin with tires still squealing and smoke streaming, says, "Now there's a guy whose dad is buying his gas and tires . . .!" Dennis and Brendan chimed in,

"You've got that right, dad!"

Kevin tearfully but clearly ended the eulogy with, "Thanks for buying our gas and tires, Dad. And thanks for being our friend."

Lee Cruise, who had worked at Bear Country, echoed the respect, love and admiration of other Bear Country employees with his eulogy:

"To a friend we care about, someone who has cared, shared, laughed and loved, someone who has been there, done that, got the tee-shirt.

"We say goodbye.

"To a friend, who, in the summer time would say, 'those weeds, it's never ending', - his love and friendship was never ending.

"To a friend, who would say, 'do the wet ones, keep the dry ones dry or do the dry ones, keep the wet ones wet', or, he would ask, 'did ya' learn anything?!'

"After knowing him, we can say, 'you bet!'

"But wait a minute, wait a minute, wait a minute, 'feed a handful of lettuce. Hang some more horns. Stay open just fifteen more minutes.'

"To a friend. 'Life is like a merry-go-round', he would say, or, 'that one looks hungry. Give him exactly this much hay.'

"To a friend who would let you go ahead and try it or tell you, 'ohhh try this. I think you're gonna like it'. We can say we have learned.

"To a friend. Through all of the wouldas, couldas, shouldas and 'yabuts', you knew he still cared, and in our good times and bad times, he didn't mind if you shared.

"To a friend we all loved.

"To a friend we all knew.

I repeat, repeat, repeat, we will all miss you."

The Mass was over. As the crowd departed Cathedral they were surprised and pleased that the sun was beginning to shine, if for only a short time. The seven Casey siblings carried their father's casket outside, led by a kilted Bagpiper. A familiar few would notice that Dennis Casey had inadvertently tucked one pant leg in his boot, something that Doc would always do. Doc was escorted to the cemetery by the Rockerville Fire Department truck and crew. Most of the mourners followed the caravan that slowly extended from the cathedral, west on Fairmont Boulevard to the stop light at Mount Rushmore Road then left, snaking up the steep grade for a few short miles until it arrived at Pine Lawn Memorial Park.

By the time the funeral caravan reached Pine Lawn, the fickle Black Hills weather changed yet again. Wispy swirls of cold steam arose from the ground and off the trees releasing the fresh smell of pine needles and new grass. After the casket was carried and placed graveside, a respectful gathering of mourners encircled the grave. From a distance, atop a grassy slope to the north, the bleating of the Highland pipes sent a collective chill through the crowd.

To the west, the ancient granite peaks of the Black Hills, framed through a stand of Ponderosa Pine, contrasted sharply with the cloud streaked South Dakota sky. Harney Peak, the highest point at over 7000 feet jutted prominently above the granite "cathedral" spires. Many of the mourners permitted their gaze to stray east, some thirty miles, where, far below, the flat Mesas of Railroad Buttes stood as pale gray sentinels on the high plains grasslands just coming into green after a long winter. The vastness and beauty eased the graveside ceremony for some if not all in attendance.

Father Zandri's closing words at the interment brought the realization to family and friends that Doc really was gone and this was to be his final home on earth. When Father Zandri finished, each member of the family walked by the casket and removed a single flower, a last tangible remembrance that would, with time, fade and dry, pressed per-haps between the pages of a book. The memories would never fade.

And then, the grandchildren walked a short distance to the hilltop, north of the grave site. At first, they were uncertain of their role in grandpa's farewell, if they really understood it was farewell. They were each handed brightly colored balloons and asked to release them up to heaven. This they did with smiling faces. Little children understand balloons far better than sickness or death or funerals. The balloons rose slowly at first, then a sudden wind pushed them up and away beyond the trees, on their journey towards the granite hills, multicolored orbs highlighted against a sky backdrop, their strings dangling casually beneath. Everyone watched until the last one, a bright red one, disappeared.

With the final wail of the Highland Pipes, the big people stepped forward to hug one another, absorbing each other's pain and strength. Little Tristin, Dennis' daughter, who was always so infatuated with Doc, came to her father's side. He picked her up and hugged her, his cheeks still wet with tears. Tristin was not too concerned about the crying. What did concern her was the fate of her balloon. "Do you think grandpa will catch mine . . .?"

Most of the mourners had departed or were slowly walking to their cars. The family, last to leave turned for a final look back to see a Native American Lakota, Dean Fairbanks, who had once worked for Doc, kneel slowly by the grave. He removed a plastic wrapper from his pocket, unwrapped it ceremoniously and poured the contents into his hand to carefully sprinkle it on top of the casket. He then arose, slowly, stood a moment more at the grave, and walked east toward the entrance to Pine Lawn Memorial Park

Dean, one of the many Native Americans who had worked for Doc, was privately paying his respects in his way to the man who had befriended him and treated him with honor and dignity as an equal. This was Dean's tribute to Doc, and a blessing enacted with a prayer to the Great Spirit. It was significant, meaningful and sincere.

Doc's children would liked to have spent more time with their Dad. There is a concern that their children, Doc's grandchildren, will never understand what a great person and a great "educator" their grandfather was. Mike Casey said, "Hopefully, some of the things that I learned from Doc, I can pass on to my sons."

Given the lessons Doc learned from his father and mother and the children of Doc learned from their father and mother, it can be safely said that the grandchildren of Dennis Patrick Casey and Pauline Foley Casey will learn, not just the sweet taste of life but also the bitter parts, the hopes, the failures and the accomplishments. Life without this blend would be, as Doc might had put it, "Damn boring

EPILOGUE

"Doc" was who he was. He was far from perfect and close to grace. An enigma. A man who lived, "Be who you are, not who you are not." His legacy does not lie wholly in his dream of the Bear Country wildlife park and the more than 7 million people who have already shared the dream seeing, animals in the wild, many for the first time. This was the result of dreaming, planning, hard work, looking to the future and taking a chance, just as anyone would with a business venture.

The legacy of Dennis Patrick Casey is fulfilled in the lives and dedicated works of Kevin, Dennis, Brendan, Sean, Shannon, Michael and John, the Casey kids, unified through family values handed down to Doc from his mother and father then passed on hand-in-hand with the understanding, patient, at times frustrated but always tolerant and cooperative love of his wife and best friend, Pauline.

Surely, there must be an Irish pub somewhere in heaven. If so, Doc and his Irish mates, old and new, are forever singing, "When Irish Eyes Are Smiling". And, as he looks down upon this dismal earth, Doc will tug at the soiled brim of his old Stetson, raise a never empty glass and toast, "Slainte" in perfect Gaelic, wink with a Leprechaun twinkle of his eye, and through that Irish Mug Grin pose the question for each of us to answer in our own way, "Did ya' learn anything . . . ?"

CASEY FAMILY HISTORY

Ancestors of Dennis Patrick Casey

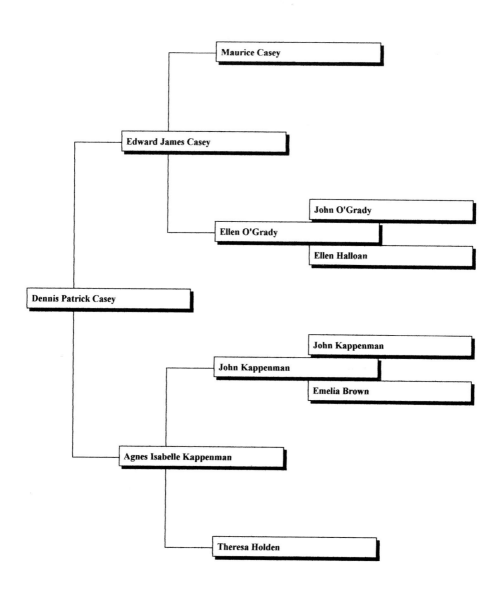

Maurice Casey

Edward James Casey

John O'Grady

Ellen O'Grady

Ellen Halloan

Dennis Patrick Casey

John Kappenman

John Kappenman

Emelia Brown

Agnes Isabelle Kappenman

Theresa Holden

Descendants of Dennis Patrick Casey

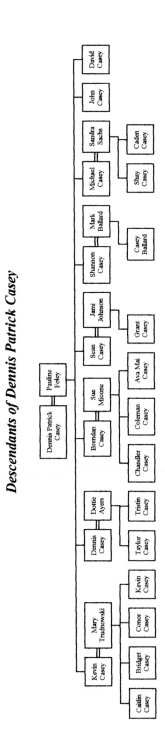

Descendants of John O'Grady

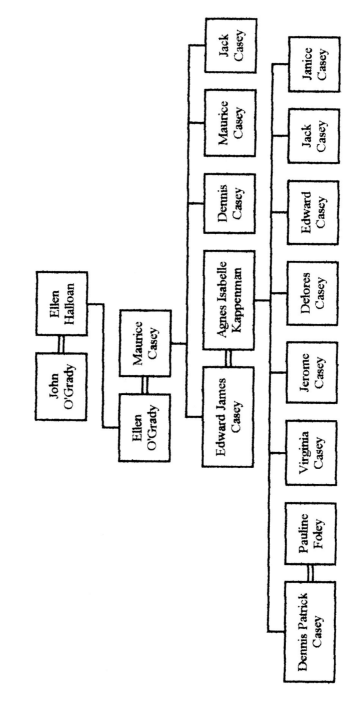

Descendants of Maurice Casey

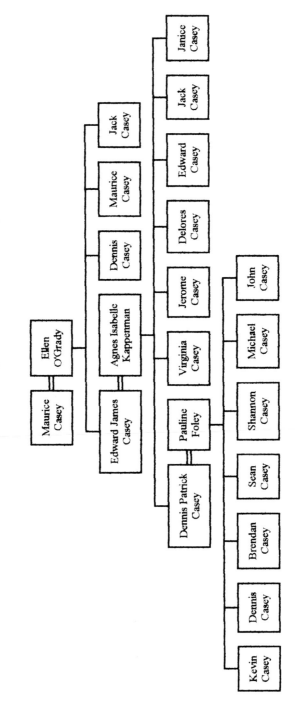

Descendants of John Kappenman

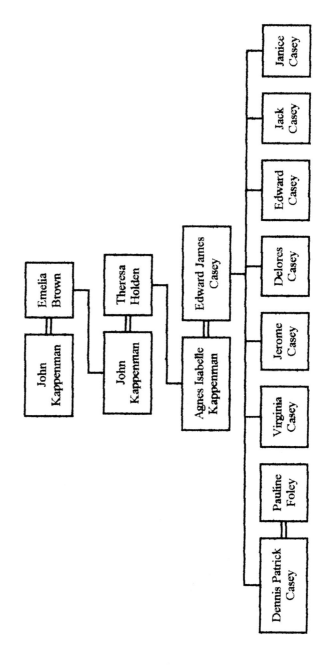

THE AUTHOR

Don Theye lives with his wife, Dort, in the Black Hills of South Dakota. Since 1969, he has shared his poetry and music in schools and colleges throughout America. He is a life-member of the International Ski for Light and has been actively involved since 1980 with the Black Hills Regional Ski for Light, which provides winter and summer outdoor activities for visually impaired and physically challenged participants.

For his pioneering efforts in the use of poetry as a therapeutic tool with psychiatric patients, Don was awarded a special certification as a Poetry Therapist from the Association of Poetry Therapy in 1979. During a two year pilot program with a mental health center, he wrote, "You Can't Rhyme All the Thyme" a manual of Poetry Therapy techniques.

Some of his honors include: Three Freedom Foundation George Washington Honor Medals, Outstanding Virginia author for his musical drama, "Wind, Needle and Star", American Song Festival, recognition for contemporary literary achievement from Cambridge, and a New York Poetry Forum award for his poem, "Ed", on inter-racial brotherhood. He is an associate member of the Academy of American Poets.

He has published six other books and authored articles in various magazines. With the encouragement of his friend, Jon Crane, the nationally recognized artist, Don is painting watercolors himself. In 1997, he was invited to do a one-man show of 50 paintings in Norway.

Don was also Jon Crane's business manager for several years.